A WOR...
DIFFE...

THE BIG GREEN P...

Recycle, Recycle, Recycle! Love the world you live in. Be good to your planet. Don't be mean, be green! Recycle, Recycle, Recycle! Love the world you live in. Be good to your planet. Don't be mean, be green! Recycle, Recycle, Recycle! Love the world you live in. Be good to your planet. Don't be mean, be green! Recycle, Recycle, Recycle! Love the

Eastern Poets

Edited by Annabel Cook

First published in Great Britain in 2009 by:

Young Writers
Remus House
Coltsfoot Drive
Peterborough
PE2 9JX
Telephone: 01733 890066
Website: www.youngwriters.co.uk

Book Design by Ali Smith & Tim Christian

SB ISBN 978-1-84924-025-3

Foreword

Young Writers' A World of Difference is a showcase for our nation's most brilliant young poets to share their thoughts, hopes and fears for the planet they call home.

Young Writers was established in 1990 to nurture creativity in our children and young adults, to give them an interest in poetry and an outlet to express themselves. Seeing their work in print will encourage them to keep writing as they grow, and become our poets of tomorrow.

Selecting the poems has been challenging and immensely rewarding. The effort and imagination invested by these young writers makes their poems a pleasure to enjoy reading time and time again.

Contents

Woodlands School, Basildon

The Poems

It All Adds Up

Less cars,
More bikes.
Less planes,
More birds.
Fewer concrete jungles,
More rainforests.
Fewer supermarkets,
More markets.
Less coal,
Less oil,
Less pollution!
More trees,
More air;
Back to nature!

Darius de Boer (13)

Waste In War

Food, food, strewn across the floor,
Food fighting in a war.
The burgers are amassing,
The turkey is crashing,
The nuggets are flying,
The kebabs are dying.
Food, food, strewn across the floor,
Food, food spinning everywhere.
Food, food flying without care,
The biscuits, *crunch!*
They make a mess of lunch.
The fries are screaming,
The soup is steaming.
Food, food, spinning everywhere,
Food, food, spinning everywhere.
Never waste food,
It is never good.
Don't get rough and tough
And ensure all the world's stuff.

Alexander Tsang (11)
Colchester Royal Grammar School, Colchester

Nature's Voice

The world is being devastated
From what humans could've stopped.
The creatures of the land are damaged
The plants wither in shock.

Nature howls into the still of night
Asking for mercy from us
But we just point and laugh in her face
Breaking her loyal trust.

Tornadoes, hurricanes she brings here
Earthquakes destroying masses.
A flood she will bring our world
We'll bear painful lashes.

But among our twisted nations
Are the charitable few
Who do her a devoted favour
Whom assist me and you.

Rainforests shatter under our word
From our forgetful race
The snow lands thaw from their icy shells
Cracking us from our cold case.

A flood it will bring and also despair
Drowning from our dire fate
Unless we take action here and now
It will be too late.

So think about our Mother Nature
And then see what you can do.
Maybe you can make a difference
And maybe all of us too.

If the world is being ravaged
From what humans could've sopped.
The creatures of the land will live
And restore what the world has got.

Life.

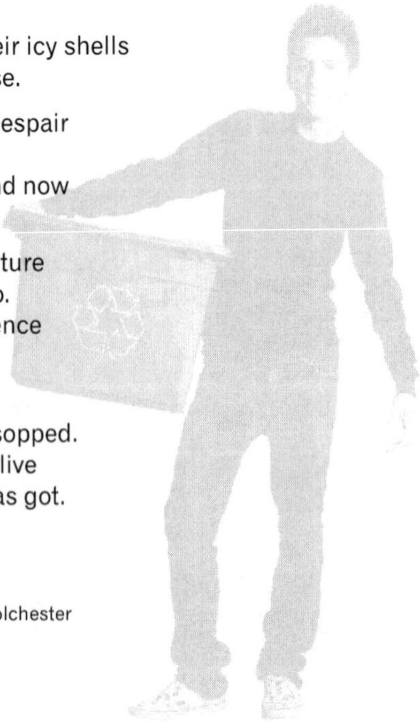

Jason Goss (11)
Colchester Royal Grammar School, Colchester

Michael's Tale

There was a boy, his name was Michael
And he never did recycle.
Now we all know it is a sin
Just to put everything in the bin.
But little Mike just shoved it in
Paper, fruit peel, glass and tin.
Now all this stuff you should recycle
But that had not occurred to Michael.
He got it all and chucked it in
So then he needed a bigger bin.
The next bin was the size of a table
Mike filled it as much as he was able.
And after everything had gone in
Yes, Mike needed a bigger bin!
An elephant could have sat in Mike's next bin
But instead he filled it with glass and tin.
And after the cardboard had gone in
Michael needed a bigger bin!
The garden was filled by the next one
But Mike didn't care what he had done.
That night, a terrible storm raged through town
Turning cars to rubble, knocking houses down.
The ear-splitting noise woke Michael up
And he saw by his bed his plastic cup.
Glancing out of his window he saw the bin
And he realised he had to put the cup in.
He put on his slippers and dressing gown
And jumped out of the window going down and down.
He hit the grass with a massive thud
And helplessly rolled into a puddle of mud.
The icy wind was harsh and cruel
Freezing Michael in his little mud pool.
But worse was to come, the bin toppled over
Michael tried looking for a four-leaf clover.
But flat as a pancake was Michael's fate
And his gravestone marker bears today's date.

Sam Hopkins (11)
Colchester Royal Grammar School, Colchester

Energy

We use a lot of energy
Throughout the day and night.
With fossil fuels running out
This surely can't be right.

So can you make energy
Any other way?
There must be other options
That can power us someday.

We could make solar energy
From the sun's rays.
Just one day of sunshine
Could last a home for days.

We could make energy from the wind
As long as there is weather.
And from what scientists believe
That will last forever.

Perhaps energy from the waves
Could be another way.
We just have to wait for the tide
Which happens twice a day.

There's also nuclear energy
That could supply our needs.
If we could make it safer
We'd be energy rich indeed.

So maybe in the future
Man will be able to say,
'We can make renewable energy
In a cheap and harmless way!'

Robert Martin (11)
Colchester Royal Grammar School, Colchester

Think

Think before you toss that packet
Think before you drop that can
Think before you tip that takeaway
And decide the best thing that you can.

Think before you make that insult
Think before you say that word
Think before you shout that curse
And decide the best way to be heard.

Think before you shred that cardboard
Think before you trash that paper
Think before you smash that glass
And decide how it could be used later.

Think before you take that journey
Think before you drive that car
Think before you start that engine
And decide if you need to go that far.

Think before you take that belonging
Think before you spoil that day
Think before you land that punch
And decide if you would like to feel that way.

Think when you see that charity
Think when you see that cause
Think when you see that meaning
And decide if that thing really needs more.

Think about this world around you
And decisions you make every day
And decide if you can make this world around us
A better place every single day.

Sebastian Marshall (11)
Colchester Royal Grammar School, Colchester

Mission: Impossible?

Place: Beijing China – Problem: smog
Cloud covering the sky line
Masked people in the hustle and bustle
Cause: boxes on wheels
Choking the Earth.

Place: Middle East – Problem: war
Dry, dead land
Victim to a futile cause
All hope taken for its people
An argument gone too far.

Place: South America – Problem: deforestation
Trees, hundreds of years old
Cut down without a second thought
Short term gains, long term losses
Dust where once life teemed.

Place: Polar regions – Problem: melting ice caps
The world's thermostat stuck on high
Giant ice cubes in the sea
Water everywhere rising
Land disappearing, climate changing.

Your mission, should you choose to accept it
Clear skies
World peace
Green not greed
Save energy

Save the world!

Dominic Blanchard (12)
Colchester Royal Grammar School, Colchester

Reptilian Rubbish

Litter engulfs the poisoned city like a snake, it wraps itself around the world,
The snake rustles as its many scales of crisp packets and other debris.
A gust of wind blows the coiled reptile into a mournful heap of trash.
The garbage lies forgotten and forlorn, forgotten by time.

Finn Holyroyd (11)
Colchester Royal Grammar School, Colchester

Rainforest

Habitat destroyer
Axe wielder
Chainsaw holder
Digger driver
Helmet wearer
Saw user
Landscape changer
Wood burner
Money maker
Soil eroder
Log seller
Life ender.

Awe inspirer
Oxygen giver
Carbon dioxide taker
Climate keeper
Ground coverer
Tree grower
Food supplier
Shelter maker
Nature preserver
Tribe hider
Nest holder
Life provider.

James Bloodworth (11)
Colchester Royal Grammar School, Colchester

Killing Planet Earth

If we can't stop acid rain
Then all the forests will go down the drain.
And if we don't stop burning oil
This beautiful planet we will spoil.
And if we can't stop using our car
Then the pollution will have gone too far.
So if we can't stop polluting the air
People will die, then we might care.

Andrew Waddingham (11)
Colchester Royal Grammar School, Colchester

Street Life

The smell of freshly baked bread
The comfort of a warm bed
The warmth of a crackling fire
The sound of ticking clocks
The smell of steaming hot meals
The comfort of tender hands
The warmth of snuggling cats
The sound of laughter . . .
Dreams . . .

Home sweet home.

The smell of litter and rubbish
The discomfort of a concrete floor
The coldness of a blustery wind
The sound of chattering people
The smell of dropped cigarettes
The discomfort of cardboard blankets
The coldness of wet damp clothes
The sound of busy people's footsteps
Too busy, too busy to care
Nightmares . . .

Home street home.

Joe Archer (11)
Colchester Royal Grammar School, Colchester

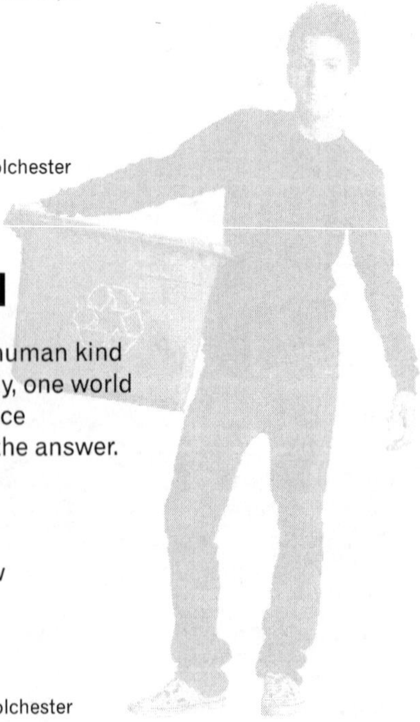

War Is Truly Evil

War is an embarrassment to human kind
We are one species, one family, one world
We should live in unity, in peace
Death and destruction is not the answer.
Dying, crying, sighing, lying
Life on Earth has hit a low
Time to end this brutal show.
We could live in peace, I know
It's definite, war has to go
Please stop now!

Joseph Peacock (11)
Colchester Royal Grammar School, Colchester

One Voice

We have a chance
We have a choice
Let's work together
All with one voice.

It is our actions
That causes this pollution
We are the ones
Causing animals' extinction.

Waste leads to poverty
Think before you buy
We can all recycle more
Come on, let's give it a try.

Let's learn from our mistakes
Let's keep these beautiful lands
We are the future
It's all in our hands.

We have a chance
We have a choice
Let's work together
All with one voice.

Robert Parry (11)
Colchester Royal Grammar School, Colchester

World Peace

W ars devastate our planet
O ur beautiful world is slowly dying
R ainforests and forests cut down while animals suffer
L ittle creatures the squirrels get hit by a car's buffer
D oing all this makes peace very hard to achieve

P eace is not impossible if we act fast
E nvironment saved from nasty things of the past
A nimals are protected because hunting is banned
C an everyone help? Of course they can!
E veryone's help is what we need to save this most amazing world.

Lahiru Munasinghe (11)
Colchester Royal Grammar School, Colchester

Litter, Litter Everywhere

Litter makes me feel
Angry and unreal.
On the floor I find
People being so unkind.

Litter, litter everywhere,
Why do so few people care?

Now look, I've found some gum on my feet,
What an unpleasant treat.
Isn't the grass meant to be green?
Under the rubbish it can't be seen!

Litter, litter everywhere,
Why do so few people care?

So if you all do just one thing
And put your litter in the bin,
Then we can put a stop to this,
Surely it can't be just *my* wish?

Litter, litter everywhere,
Why do so few people care?

Ben Shergold (11)
Colchester Royal Grammar School, Colchester

By Global Warming

The world is heating up
By global warming.
Icebergs are melting
By global warming.
Gases pollute the air
By global warming.
Rubbish is heaping up
By global warming.
Everything is dying
By global warming.
We can all help
To *stop* global warming.

Ben Orbell (11)
Colchester Royal Grammar School, Colchester

A Grandson's Wish

My gran tells me that when she was a child,
Winters were cold and summers were mild.
Everyone knew what seasons would bring,
Falling leaves in autumn, flowers in spring.
Now the seasons have lost their way
We barbecue in October and build snowmen in May!
All over the world things are going wrong
And scientists say it won't be long
Before it's too late to save our planet.
We all need to do just a little bit
If everyone did we could put it right
So let us be green with all our might.
Let's switch off our lights, turn down the gas,
Recycle our paper, plastic and glass.
Buy local produce and grow our own veg,
If gardens are small, use the window ledge.
Try not to drive our cars every day,
Let's ride our bikes to keep CO_2 at bay.
Earth can be saved if we worked together,
Then our grandchildren can see Grandma's weather.

William McMahon (11)
Colchester Royal Grammar School, Colchester

Help Earth

H is for help, the call from our desperate planet,
E is for everyone can help just by recycling,
L is for litter, litter which can be recycled,
P is for pollution destroying the ice caps and causing global warming.

E is for extinction, extinction of the animals and rainforest, once so plentiful,
A is for accusing, this is our job to clean up our poor Earth,
R is for reuse, reuse, reduce, recycle all these things we can do,
T is for time, time is running out for us to save our planet,
H is for healthy, what our planet needs, healthy air,
Healthy sun and healthy sea, all of which can help our planet be saved.

Freddy Billowes (12)
Colchester Royal Grammar School, Colchester

Sammy Orang-Utan Says, 'Save The Rainforest'

Hi, I'm Sammy who lives in the Amazon
I'm afraid you humans are a con.
What have we animals done to you?
And still this is what you do.
You cut our trees, you disturb our home,
You leave us survivors all alone.
You make us die, our numbers decrease,
But still you never ever cease.
Insects, birds and animals alike,
You say to us, 'On your bike!'
Gradually we are forced away
Closer to extinction every day.
Soon we beautiful creatures shall be gone
So our voices call out as one.
No longer should our habitat fuel your needs,
To compensate your damage, plant more seeds.
So in the future we will be
Living happily for all to see.

Tom Fadden (11)
Colchester Royal Grammar School, Colchester

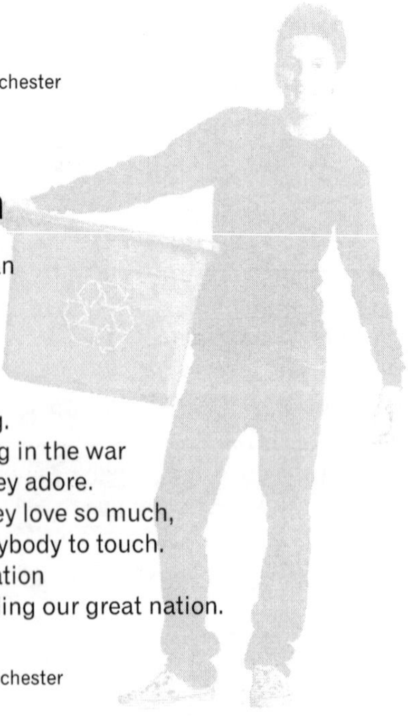

The Quiet Green

If you're thinking of being mean
Don't, be green!
Pick that litter up off the floor,
Put it in the bin next door.
Turn down the heating,
It's warm out, so stop cheating.
Think about the people fighting in the war
Risking their lives for those they adore.
All the people at home that they love so much,
The people they don't want anybody to touch.
So in quiet times of contemplation
Think about the people defending our great nation.

Joseph Logan (11)
Colchester Royal Grammar School, Colchester

Johnny Whitter From Mean To Green

Once upon a time lived Johnny Whitter
Who was a devilish little critter,
But at recycling he was a quitter
Because he always dropped his litter.
To him recycling was a waste of time,
He didn't consider it a crime
Until one day in a dream,
Lack of recycling turned him green!
When he woke up, he gave a sigh,
Until his mother gave a cry.
When she said, 'My, oh my!'
He realised it was not a lie.
And now the truth was plain to see,
He was as green as the leaves on a tree.
So planet Earth had decided to punish
Johnny, for not dealing with his rubbish.
So remember, put it in the bin
Unless it's paper, plastic, glass or tin.

Lewis Tuthill (11)
Colchester Royal Grammar School, Colchester

Animal Extinction

Animals becoming less and less every day
For example tigers getting shot while they play.

In times of need
Poachers come in greed.

In great numbers they come
Through woods of lumber with guns.

Animals being held in zoos
A lot of people and me give it thumbs down and boo.

Our sons will not see
How sad the creatures be.

So if we do nothing about it
The animals will never be free!

Benjamin Graham (11)
Colchester Royal Grammar School, Colchester

Recycle

Bottle, cans, give them a rinse
Recycling makes a lot of sense.
Newspapers, cardboard, papers galore
Magazines, comics, recycle more.

Stop the landfills from filling up
All you need is a clean up.
Don't throw things away
Just recycle to protect the highway.

Look after the Earth that we live on
Recycle before the Earth is gone.
Put your rubbish out for the recycling van
Or in the winter you won't be able to build a snowman.

Cherish the Earth we share
And with your rubbish take care.
Recycle to use things again
To avoid having a handful the size of Big Ben.

Ryan Collins (12)
Colchester Royal Grammar School, Colchester

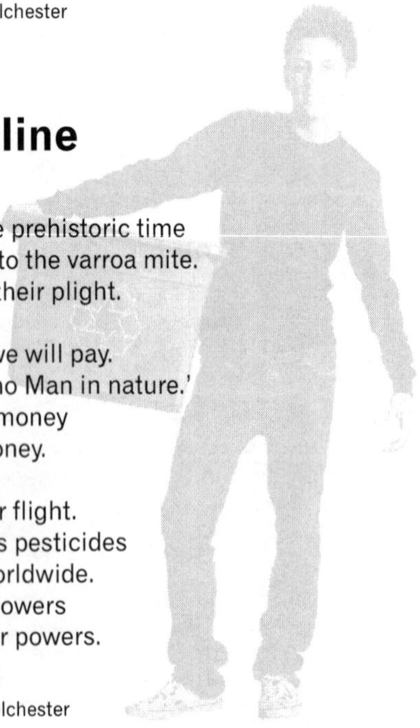

Bees Are In Decline

The bees are in decline
They've been pollinating since prehistoric time
But now bees are falling prey to the varroa mite.
Mankind should be fearful of their plight.
As Einstein said one day,
'If bees become extinct then we will pay.
For four years later they'll be no Man in nature.'
DEFRA needs to spend more money
So the bees can make their honey.
Research into the varroa mite
So the bees can continue their flight.
Less mobile phone masts, less pesticides
So plants continue to grow worldwide.
Everyone should plant more flowers
So the bees can maintain their powers.

Charlie Ridley-Johnson (11)
Colchester Royal Grammar School, Colchester

Act Now

I am floating amongst slabs of ice
Lost in a blizzard of snow
This is for a reason however
The ice is melting you know.

Along comes a fishing trawler
Catching all the fish
My family is starving
To feed them is my only wish.

Another tree falls
The rainforest looks meeker
As the bulldozer draws nearer
Our future looks bleaker.

We have to be more careful
Before it's too late
We have to act now
To avoid their fate.

Joshua Read (11)
Colchester Royal Grammar School, Colchester

Bin It!

Don't drop your litter
Or you'll be feeling quite bitter if you do.
Litter is everything
Remember that because quite a lot don't.
Just keep it within
Until you find a bin
Then have no hesitation and put it in.
It's a sin if you don't
Cos if you do you're a killer
For every plastic bag dropped
If you're a bird that's the chop.
Finally don't drop your gum
Why? You'll suffocate a bee.
I hope you'll take on board what I've said
And not be responsible for another animal dead!

Abraham Bickersteth (12)
Colchester Royal Grammar School, Colchester

Johnny Smith

Have you head about little Johnny Smith?
Believe me this story is no myth.
Every time he's walking in the street
He drops paper, tissues and even sweets.

His mum's always telling him, 'Johnny, don't drop litter,
Walk to that bin, it'll make you fitter.'
But Johnny's too busy dropping litter to listen to his mum
And gobbling sweets to fill his tum.

In Johnny's house the bins had barely been filled
Except for cans of Coke which had already been chilled.
The house was a mess and everybody knew
With bits of tissue and sweet wrappers too.

But one day Johnny walked over to his bin
He tripped on something and suddenly he fell in!
The bin men came and took him away
That was the price he had to pay.

James Roberts (11)
Colchester Royal Grammar School, Colchester

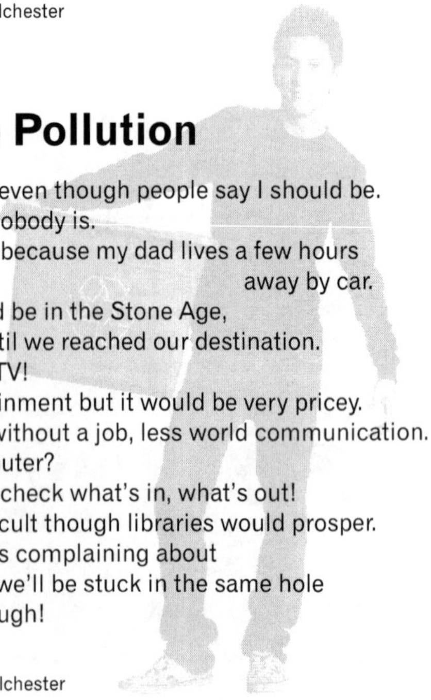

If There Was No Pollution

I have to admit, I'm not green even though people say I should be.
But when you think about it, nobody is.
We can't be green completely because my dad lives a few hours away by car.
But if we didn't have cars we'd be in the Stone Age,
Trekking for days and days until we reached our destination.
Think about if we didn't have TV!
I know there would be entertainment but it would be very pricey.
There would be more people without a job, less world communication.
What if we didn't have a computer?
There would be no Internet to check what's in, what's out!
Life would be much more difficult though libraries would prosper.
So I don't see what everyone is complaining about
Until we discover some more we'll be stuck in the same hole
Don't think that'll be soon though!

Edward Bloor (11)
Colchester Royal Grammar School, Colchester

It's All Down To Us

The world's dying and it's all down to us,
But no one's stopping and packing their stuff.
So let's shut up that window, turn off the light
'Cause if we don't we're in for a fright!

The world's dying and it's all down to us,
But no one's stopping and packing their stuff.
So let's take a quick shower instead of a bath
And when everything's fine we can all have a laugh.

The world's dying and it's all down to us,
But no one's stopping and packing their stuff.
So let's turn down that thermo, throw on a fleece
And maybe the ice caps will stop melting at least!

The world's dying and it's all down to us,
But no one's stopping and packing their stuff.
No time to procrastinate, bicker or row
We need to take action so do something now!

Calum Mills (11)
Colchester Royal Grammar School, Colchester

The Polar Bear

As I awake, I feel the morning sun's rays boring into me,
like a never-ending gaze
But as I arise and stretch out my strong white legs,
I sense something is wrong, that there is trouble ahead
I continue and glance up at my family, still slumbering on their icy bed,
After all, a bear must keep his family well fed.
I shudder but suddenly I stumble and hear a crack and see the ice crumble!
Alarmed, I see fear in my wife's eyes and in my cubs, confusion and surprise
I tear across the ice, my heart breaking inside,
I am too late and I watch my family drift into the sun's watery gates
And as I sit on the ice with a tear in my eye, I look up at the sun
and then I know why.

Jasper Reid (11)
Colchester Royal Grammar School, Colchester

Earth

The Earth is crying out for help
So help it to repair
It needs your help to carry on
So it doesn't disappear.

Pollution forges acid rain
Which pours for quite a while
It turns blue to grey every day
And makes the cold ice boil.

The cars, the planes and buses
Create evil living clouds
That spend all day rising up
To form some flying shrouds.

So help the world and start today
Recycle all your things
Get out your bike that's in the shed
So a better future begins.

Freddy Whitten (11)
Colchester Royal Grammar School, Colchester

Extinction

Each day something, somewhere, is becoming extinct.
Humans are destroying the Earth,
And with each new species that becomes extinct,
We are taking a step backwards towards our own demise.

Humans are Nature's only mistake.
They are destroying themselves
As they are destroying all other things.
Soon their end will come, when they are destroyed by their own stupidity.

When they are gone, the Earth will find peace, but not before
For only when humans have left the Earth,
Can it repair itself, can it begin again.
Extinction is forever and for all.

Theodore Tamblyn (11)
Colchester Royal Grammar School, Colchester

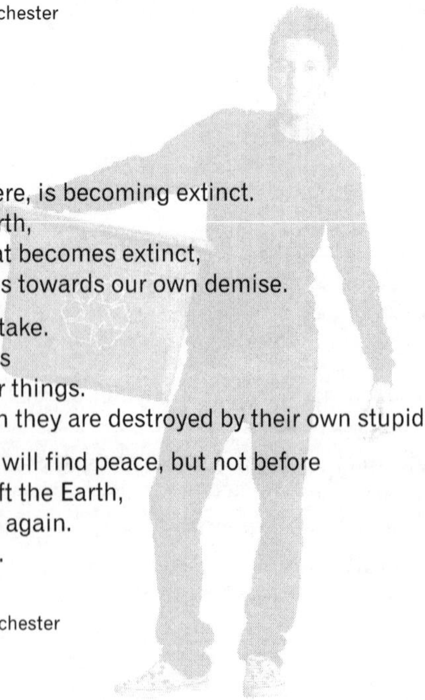

Pollution

Polluting the seas
Polluting the air
Polluting the trees
Everywhere.

Trees in the forest
Standing tall
Hear them creak
As they fall.

The ozone layer
A lot stronger than me
Is weaker than
We think it should be.

The gases we're emitting
From aeroplanes and cars
Are giving the ozone layer
Dangerous scars.

Conor Robert Mitchell (11)
Colchester Royal Grammar School, Colchester

War

War tears the world apart
It brings families so far apart
So many countries shoot to kill
Please, please not come but I know it will.

Many die every day
For the rest they all pray
Let's all hope the war ends today,
Today!

War turns man against man
Gun to gun
In a war that may never be won.
War brings tears, tears the world apart
It brings families so far apart.

Matthew Parker (11)
Colchester Royal Grammar School, Colchester

Time To Take Action

The ozone layer's ripping
And the planet's climate's high
And if we don't start learning
Acid will fall from the sky.

The polar bears are fleeing
Though there's no more ice to live on
And by 2013, if we don't change
They'll be living up in Heaven.

So let's get up from that old couch
And turn off the PlayStation!
Instead let's stroll around the park
And make a greener nation.

Let's recycle our milk bottles
And say no to 4 x 4s.
For a brighter better future
Is just outside the door.

Tom Tanner (11)
Colchester Royal Grammar School, Colchester

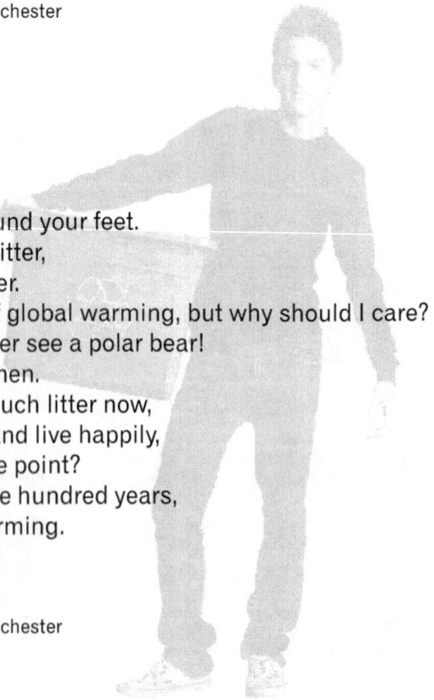

Litter

When you go out in the street,
You might find something around your feet.
It's dirty, unclean and is very bitter,
It's rubbish, also known as litter.
The planet is dying because of global warming, but why should I care?
So what, some people will never see a polar bear!
I don't care, I will be dead by then.
But if we all put a stop to so much litter now,
Others can enjoy their future and live happily,
But if we don't, then what's the point?
The planet will be dead in three hundred years,
So recycle and stop global warming.
Now, hurry, before it's too late!

Darius Azarmi (11)
Colchester Royal Grammar School, Colchester

A Better World

Air pollution, what's the solution?
Endless war, what's it for?

Climate change, greenhouse gases
Carbon footprint, teach the masses.

Black or white, rich or poor,
We are equal in God's law.

Feed the world and cure infection
Keep our rainforest and animal protection.

Keep it green to make us clean
Recycle all that can be seen.

Help the homeless, give them more
Give them shelter and a front door.

So help make the world a better place
For animals, creatures and the human race.

Ashley Webb (11)
Colchester Royal Grammar School, Colchester

Being Homeless

There is a chill in the wind and frost on the windows, I have a sleeping
sack to cower in.
Hundreds, thousands of healthy faces go past every day
One chap had a thick fur coat on and you could hear the clinking of
money in his pockets
And the tapping of the expensive leather shoes.
Walking past many a house, looking through the window
And the window showing happy families at their nice warm meals.
I can almost remember the feeling of a warm fire,
The safety and security of a nice cosy bedroom.
At Christmas the smell of delicious roasted turkey is almost overwhelming,
Life is difficult and tough but in the end it's a privilege to be alive.

Lachlan McKessar (11)
Colchester Royal Grammar School, Colchester

Hi, I'm A Polar Bear

Hi, I'm a polar bear
And I've got a complaint.
I know of you humans
And subtle you ain't!
The gases from your cars
Are eating the ozone,
The sun comes through harder
And melts my home.

I'm getting kinda hot
Under my hair,
And I'll keep getting warmer,
Don't you care?
You gotta stop polluting
Starting today.
The ice'll stop melting
And I'll be OK!

Angus Ruddick (11)
Colchester Royal Grammar School, Colchester

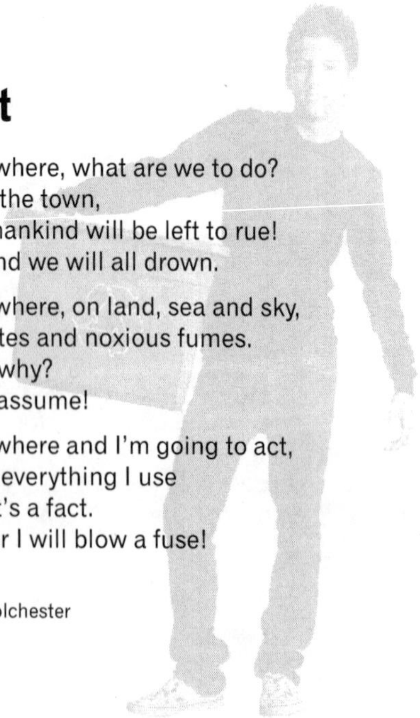

Save Our Planet

Pollution, pollution, it's everywhere, what are we to do?
In the country, in the city and the town,
If we continue in the future, mankind will be left to rue!
The polar ice caps will melt and we will all drown.

Pollution, pollution, it's everywhere, on land, sea and sky,
Plastic bags, tin cans, cigarettes and noxious fumes.
We have to question, why, oh why?
No one gets the message we assume!

Pollution, pollution, it's everywhere and I'm going to act,
I will make sure that I recycle everything I use
Before I leave this planet, that's a fact.
If I see anybody dropping litter I will blow a fuse!

Augustus Veasey (11)
Colchester Royal Grammar School, Colchester

It's Up To Us

40, 30, 20, 10,
Counting down the days we have left.
Unless we all pull together
To make a change today.

We can all make a change today
Or we'll all have a price to pay.
We don't really have a choice,
Everybody's got a voice.
Whether it's a celebrity or a normal man
Everybody should think, *I can.*
We cannot afford to dump any more,
The way we treat our planet is poor.
Our planet is a gift of kindness,
We cannot treat it with such blindness.
Overall, I'd like to say,
We cannot treat our gift this way.

James Lister (11)
Colchester Royal Grammar School, Colchester

The World's Murder

We're killing the world and that's a mistake
We need to be more economising.
You need to learn to give and not take
So you better start revising.

All over the world there's loads of pollution
And tonnes of stuff being chucked away.
The way to rectify it, here's a solution,
We recycle and carry on that way.

I could sit and tell you all day of changes I want to do
But instead I'll ask you to make little ones.
Like sharing a car when there's people of more than two
And that is from me to you.

Ben May (12)
Colchester Royal Grammar School, Colchester

Litters!

Litter, litter, all we do is litter.
The trash, the dirt it makes me feel quite bitter.
It piles up in all the streets, I really shouldn't dare
To say that it's all OK because that I just can't bear.

If we don't stop it will soon be as tall as the tallest tower,
We must try, we must do something, we must use manpower.
Boxes, bottles, bags and mugs, they're lying everywhere,
There's even litter managing to pollute our precious air.

Our world is now starting to cry,
If we don't watch out it will soon die.
C'mon, we can't all just be quitters,
We've got to stop these nasty litterers!

Calum Legorburu (12)
Colchester Royal Grammar School, Colchester

War

The soldiers advance, carefully they go
Across the desert wilderness with no sign of their foe.
No trees, no colour, just masses of sand.
Was that the glint of a gun or was it the sun?
Is death close at hand?
Suddenly, there's the crack of a gun,
Captain holds his chest as his life blood begins to seep
As he falls in a crumpled heap.
Then all is silent and all we can hear
Is the quiet of the desert once more.
As we mourn our captain,
This is war.

Matthew Davis (11)
Colchester Royal Grammar School, Colchester

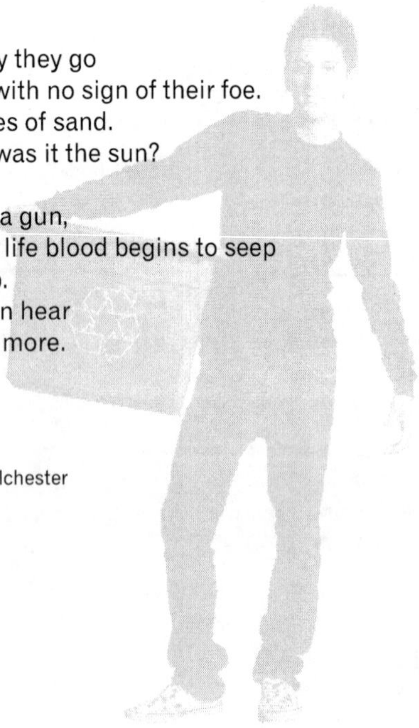

If You Want To Be Green

If you want to be green
You're going to have to clean
Up the environment
Don't be violent
To any birds
Or creatures in herds.
Recycle any can or jars
And ride a bike, don't drive your cars.
Get away from the bin
Stop chucking away
We're going to recycle
And we're starting today!

Ayrton Alexander Bourn (11)
Colchester Royal Grammar School, Colchester

Game Over?

Don't give me lines of Hope and Glory
Courage, fear and panic tell a different story.
Grasping the controls so tight in my hand
The game is warfare, the target this land.
But it isn't a game, these are real lives.
Homes for children, husbands and wives.
My orders are clear, my aim is true
But maybe these people can play the game too.
We've set the target, we scan the screen
Points for prizes, or so it seems.
Aim! Shoot! Fire! All done by remote.
A life or just points? The victim can't vote.

Sam Baker (11)
Colchester Royal Grammar School, Colchester

Don't You See?

Beneath the smog of our own doings
The Earth lies still not knowing of such things
Makes for all the worse with car and plane
When it's just as fast with bus and train

Landfills and power stations all around
As if we had the only land in town
Whatever do these generators hold
That we find to be like such gold

All the while we do not see
What misery that we create
Right outside our own front gate.

Jack Bailey (11)
Colchester Royal Grammar School, Colchester

Pollution

Pollution! Pollution! What is the solution?
I know! Don't drive a car,
That will get you very far.
Ride a bike instead,
That will get you far ahead.
Look out there, look at the sun,
Why do you keep the electric light on?
We're killing the world and ourselves as well,
Soon it will be as hot as Hell
And now that you've done all these things, just look at the world,
Just look at it sing.

Morgan Rosser (11)
Colchester Royal Grammar School, Colchester

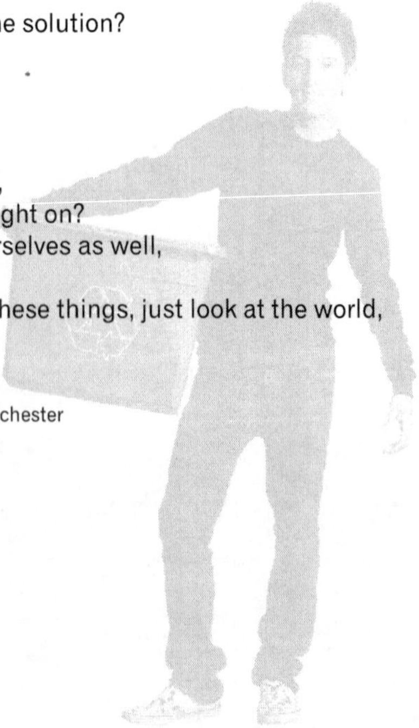

Rainforest

R ushing down, after being cut the trees fall
A ll of them living helpless creatures being murdered
I n the rainforest which are lost every day
N either being helped by us nor being left alone
F or we are gradually destroying ourselves and our planet
O xygen is needed for us; oxygen is let out by trees
R uining our planet's beauty for
E vermore, is what the crime of cutting our comrades
S o the message is this, save the
T rees and
S ave the rainforest.

Jason Joykutty (11)
Colchester Royal Grammar School, Colchester

Poverty

It's what everyone thinks about,
You all worry about the Credit Crunch!
No one thinks again about the poor
Maybe homeless, hungry, no place to go, think yourself lucky
When you sit at home on the computer or watching TV.
Why not worry about what really matters?
There are many people out there like it.
Instead of spending money on foreign DVDs,
Spend it on another person's happiness.
Even you will be proud for helping someone in need.
Do remember, it could have been you, you never know!

Ryan Kennedy (11)
Colchester Royal Grammar School, Colchester

An Inconvenient Truth - Haiku

The world is burning
The unavoidable truth
The world is dying.

Ross Brisk (11)
Colchester Royal Grammar School, Colchester

Litter

Animal killer
Water polluter
Street clutterer
Mess maker
London filler
Law breaker
Planet destroyer
Landscape hurter
Ozone destroyer
Plant remover
Just stop littering.

Gavin Burr (11)
Colchester Royal Grammar School, Colchester

Earth Needs Help

The Earth needs help, hear it cry
We need to do something or the Earth will die.
The ozone layer, depleting fast,
The Earth has not got long to last.

Climate change, is it new?
Floods and storms ice melting too.
Recycle, recycle, spread the word
Don't be stupid, it's not absurd.
We can all make a difference if we put our minds to it
So come on save the world, let's do it.

Luke Balls-Burgess (12)
Colchester Royal Grammar School, Colchester

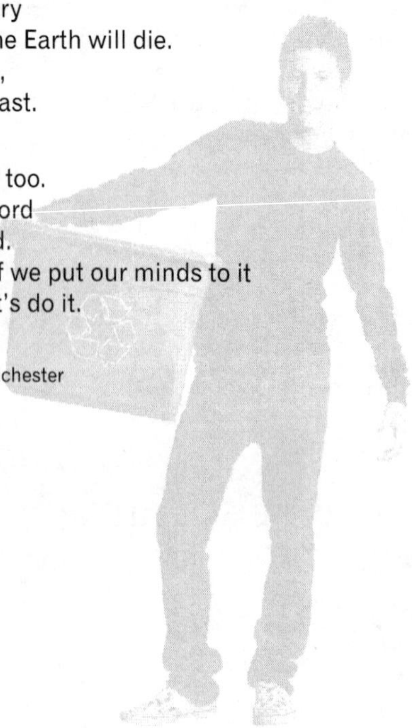

A Plastic Bag

I'm a plastic bag
Which is somewhat of a drag.
My useful life is short
Which is really not my fault.
If only someone would
Recycle and do some good.
Sustainability is the key
For plastic bags just like me.
Everybody hear my plea
And put me out of my misery!

Harry Lee (12)
Colchester Royal Grammar School, Colchester

Mother Nature - Haiku

Mother Nature sees
That we destroy this planet
For nothing at all.

Andrew Mueller (11)
Colchester Royal Grammar School, Colchester

Crime Domination

Crime is here, people are dying,
Shops are losing stock, they are lying.
The men are mad, I don't understand
But their targets can't even stand.
I'm confused, they do it on purpose,
The drug dealers sell more than one dose.
The criminals aren't nice,
They do it more than twice.
I hope they realise they've got it all wrong,
It has already been going for much too long.

Jonathan Margetts (11)
Colchester Royal Grammar School, Colchester

Rubbish!

Why is it considered such a sin
To throw your rubbish in a bin?
In our towns and cities fair
The streets would look better if they were bare.
Cigarette ends, empty packet and cans
The responsibility should be every man's.
Plastic bags are such a threat
To all wildlife and your pet.
So village, countryside, wherever you roam
Remember, *take your litter home!*

Jonathan Francis (11)
Colchester Royal Grammar School, Colchester

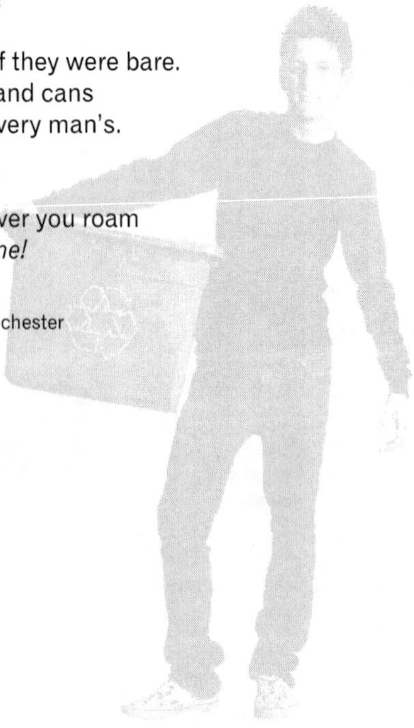

Monkey Business

R un monkeys run!
A void those poachers
I nto the trees
N ever give up
F ight for your home
O h no, here they come
R un as fast as you can
E scape with your lives
S tay hidden
T hey will return, you were lucky this time!

George Chappell (11)
Colchester Royal Grammar School, Colchester

Why Try?

Racism, why try?
It's not cool if your skin is white
Everyone's equal.

If all were the same
Skin, size, looks, thoughts, religion
What would be the point?

All other people
All have some weakness too
That's including you!

Nathan Ambury (11)
Colchester Royal Grammar School, Colchester

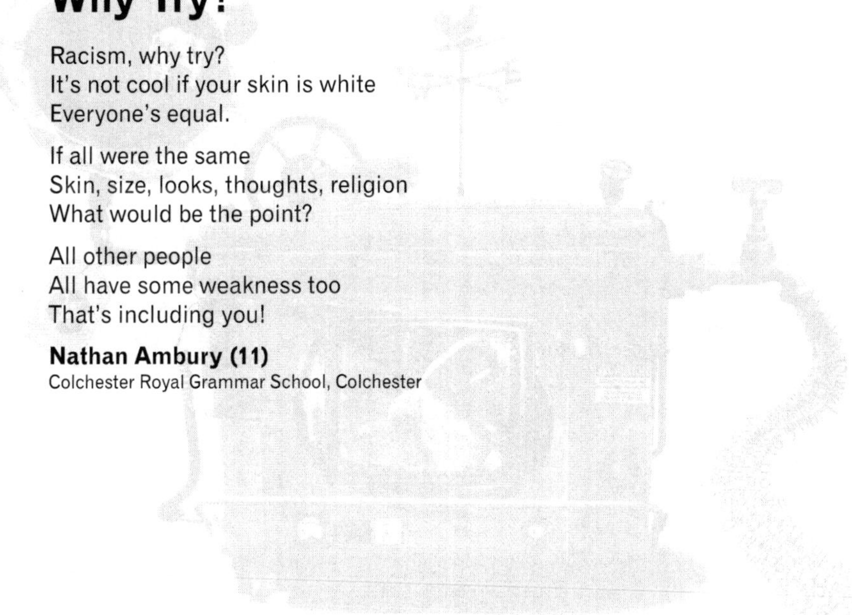

Recycle!

These days there is a lot of war
And people cutting using saws
But nearer home there's so much waste
People throw things away in haste
People who are very poor would look at our rubbish with eyes adore!

It's time to make a stand and care
And be environmentally aware
Together we can put this right
So recycle now and start tonight.

Jamie Moore (11)
Colchester Royal Grammar School, Colchester

Save Earth

S ave the planet, save our race
A nd stop the wars from taking place.
V ery rare is our home
E arth is strong, it has been shown.

E ven though we love it much
A ll of us have lost our touch.
R aining acids
T emperatures rising
H ave we any time left?

George Pertwee (12)
Colchester Royal Grammar School, Colchester

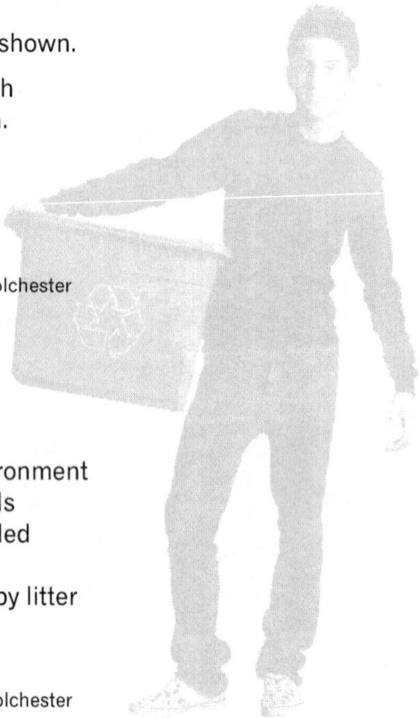

Litter

L ittering is bad for the environment
I t can be harmful to animals
T ins and cans can be recycled
T ry and do your bit
E verything can be harmed by litter
R ecycle your rubbish.

Conor Bailey (12)
Colchester Royal Grammar School, Colchester

Pollution, It's Terrible

P ollution, it's terrible
O ur lives depend on saving the world
L et pollution be abolished
L ives are treasures don't let them be lost
U nderestimation of greenhouse gases is deadly
T rying to stop pollution and saving the world is essential
I ce caps are melting, the world will flood!
O nly pure evil will stop you helping
N o one is safe, we must act now!

Adam Threlfall (11)
Colchester Royal Grammar School, Colchester

Pollution's Gonna Destroy You!

We are destroying the world it's true
And when it dies so will you!
You can flee to Mars if you like
Although Saturn's nice at this time of year,
But the only thing pollution will do is destroy you!
Wherever we go death and destruction will follow.
By the time it's Christmas we will be choking Apollo
Because it's the end of the world as we know it
And pollution's gonna destroy you, you, you!

George Eady (11)
Colchester Royal Grammar School, Colchester

Theft

Theft is not a good thing
It won't resolve a problem
And just because they're rich
Doesn't mean you have to rob them.
If it's for drugs or booze or just because you want to
Think before you do it
Cos someone's bound to see you!

Harry Wilson (11)
Colchester Royal Grammar School, Colchester

Save Our Planet

Only if everyone could understand what has gone wrong,
There is litter here and there; as a matter of fact it's everywhere!
Animals are dying out and that is without a doubt.
The ozone layer may not be there but hardly anyone actually cares.
Recycling is one of the keys to success, without it we will all be a mess.
Without the rabbits that hop and the cows that say *moo,* what would we do?
The Earth may look perfect to the human eye but one day it may die!
By recycling, shredding and putting things in the bin, we might
be able to prevent this awful thing.

Imran Ladak (11)
Colchester Royal Grammar School, Colchester

I Doubt It

Bang! Another man goes silent,
Oh why is this world so very violent?
The world is what the powerful try to dominate,
Leaving hundreds of landscapes in a horrific state.
Lives lost because of religion or race,
The killers are a *big* disgrace.
Will we ever live in peace?
Will this fighting ever cease?
I doubt it.

Robert Aherne (11)
Colchester Royal Grammar School, Colchester

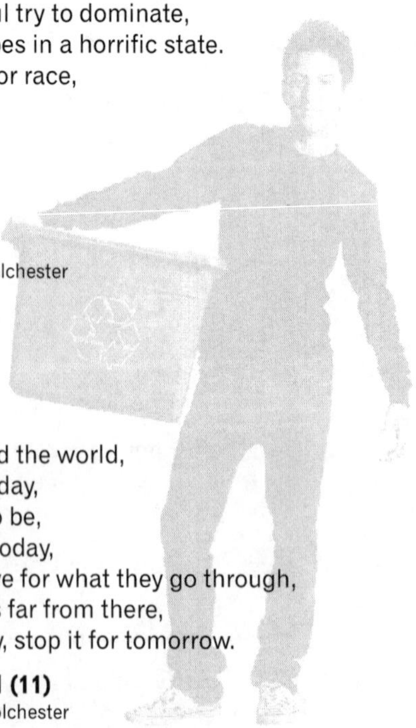

Poverty

P rotection for people around the world,
O ppression they face every day,
V ersatile is what we need to be,
E ncouraging for our youth today,
R espect is what they deserve for what they go through,
T rust in their government is far from there,
Y oung ones dying every day, stop it for tomorrow.

Zachary Campbell-Crawford (11)
Colchester Royal Grammar School, Colchester

Why?

Why do we do it?
Oh why, oh why, oh why?
Why do we drive around in shocking huge cars
Letting out emissions to our precious ozone.

Why do we kill it, make everything warm.
So I ask to all the murderers out there
Please, please, please stop it!

Rory Patterson (11)
Colchester Royal Grammar School, Colchester

Rainforests

Rainforest, our biggest friends . . . *chop!*
We are destroying them, they are giving us air to breathe and we go slaughtering them
Without these trees we all will be dead without hope or anything said.
They save us from most terrible fates and all work at incredible rates
And how do we repay them? We cut them down without so much as a tiny frown.

Thomas Illidge (11)
Colchester Royal Grammar School, Colchester

War

I am awoken with the sound of the siren wailing
Screaming, shouting, a mass of confusion.
I scramble for my gas mask, running down the stairs.
I run out to the shelter as a bomb falls nearby.
I hit the deck and wait.
Time passes slowly as I wait for the 'all clear' sign.
Finally there it is, my terror is over for another night.

Oliver Stovell (11)
Colchester Royal Grammar School, Colchester

Climate Destruction

C rime, it happens on the streets.
L itter, it covers the world.
I ce, it is melting into water.
M en, they're heading off to war.
A nimals, they are slowly becoming extinct.
T rees, they're being chopped down.
E nvironment, it's changing for the worse.

Jack Taylor (11)
Colchester Royal Grammar School, Colchester

Pollution

The world was beautiful before it came
If only things were still the same.
The world has changed ever so much
If only things were still as such.
Some places are worse than others
Especially where it smothers
It's called pollution!

Jake Allen (11)
Colchester Royal Grammar School, Colchester

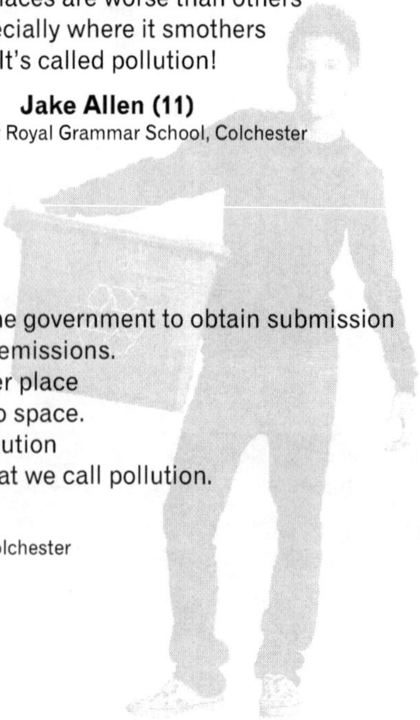

Pollution

We need to put pressure on the government to obtain submission
To reduce the world's carbon emissions.
Let's make our world a happier place
And not lose all our gases into space.
We urgently need to find a solution
With the great big problem that we call pollution.

Alex Green (11)
Colchester Royal Grammar School, Colchester

Change

I look around me at the world today
And I wonder how it will be when I'm old and grey.
The weather at the moment is really strange
And it's all to do with climate change.
I wonder more about being old and grey
Will there be a world for my children to play?

Calum Davy (11)
Colchester Royal Grammar School, Colchester

Save Our Planet

How the Earth is dying,
It pains me to see
How people are always lying
Saying, 'It isn't down to me!'

I look up to the clouds
And watch them float right by,
The cars drive by so loud
And it's then I wonder why.

The Earth has always been here
And we want it here to stay,
So just stop and listen, hear
How the animals talk and play.

If you ever have a moment
Then think what you could do
To the forests that are absent
Of animals, now in the zoo.

If you do something soon enough
Then I think that you should know
That although the Earth is tough,
This planet we inhabit will be as dead as a dodo.

Rebecca Turvey (14)
Hastingsbury Business & Enterprise College, Kempston

Do You?

You think you're deprived, do you?
You don't get what you see, do you?
Do you care about Africa, do you?
I didn't think so.

Different environments all over the world,
Some better, some worse, I'm told.
Africa, Asia, Europe, South America
War-torn, poverty, I heard.

People queuing for water, is that you?
Bare feet cut, is that you?
Children working dawn till dusk, is that you?
I didn't think so.

Different environments all over the world,
Some better, some worse, I'm told.
Africa, Asia, Europe, South America,
Dying, disease, I heard.

Thinner and thinner, do you want that?
On the streets, no money, do you want that?
Baking, no food, do you want that?
I didn't think so.

Different environments all over the world,
Some better, some worse, I'm told.
Africa, Asia, Europe, South America,
Suffering, no hope, I heard.

Do you want to do something, do you?
Sponsor a family, do you?
Give a little of the lot you have, do you?
Yes, I thought so!

Roisin McErlean (13)
Hastingsbury Business & Enterprise College, Kempston

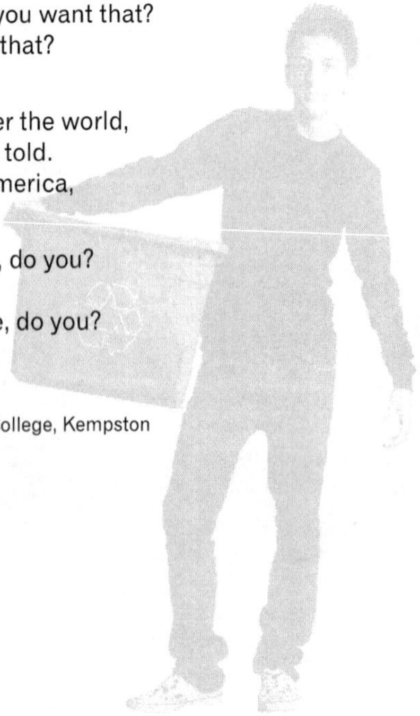

Everywhere Floods

E verywhere there's a flood
V ets and pets all destroyed
E nd of the world with water
R ain, rain, please go away
Y ucky muddy floors
W ater, water everywhere
H umans screaming and shouting
E veryone help the people
R arely any services here
E ngines come and help

F ire-fighters to the rescue
L ift everyone from here
O ver there is fire as well
O ver here people getting hired and fired
D rowning people
S inking away, everyone is dead
because everywhere there are floods!

E veryone save the flood
M others get your children
E veryone save the world
R ushing floors with water
G et the services
E veryone save the flood
N o water should be here
C are for your people and
Y ou will be saved.

Alisha Dhanda (13)
Hastingsbury Business & Enterprise College, Kempston

Kempston Flood

In Kempston there was a flood
And under the flood there was mud.
The villagers had to start thinking
Before they started sinking
So they started to shout 'Oh crud!'

Jake Handscomb (13)
Hastingsbury Business & Enterprise College, Kempston

Flood

The water came in
Levels started to rise,
She could hear all the shouting,
Hear all the cries.

She got deeper and deeper
As the water came in,
What was she to do
For she could not swim?

Down she went
Under the water,
Is this right,
Nature's way of slaughter?

But then she came up,
Back up to the top,
A lifejacket she put on
Which she'd bought from the shop.

That lifejacket helped
For now she lives,
So glad that she bought it,
Saved her life it did.

Alesha Kali-Rai (14)
Hastingsbury Business & Enterprise College, Kempston

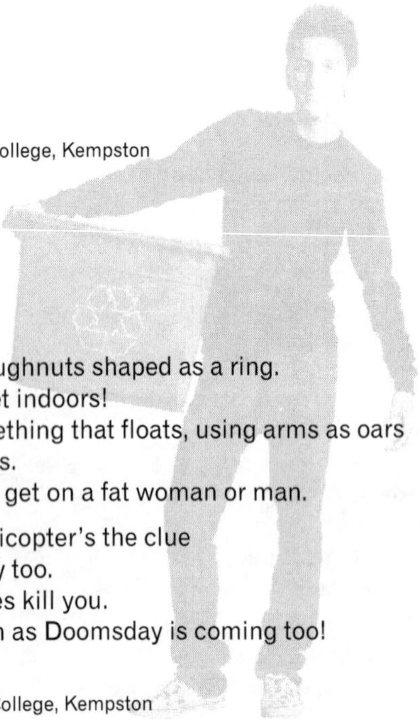

Aqua

At 6am Kempston's flooding,
People are stocking up on doughnuts shaped as a ring.
The aqua is coming, quick, get indoors!
Kids and families get on something that floats, using arms as oars
But let the OAPs use the boats.
If you have nothing but a can, get on a fat woman or man.

Prepare for the rescue the helicopter's the clue
So get in and on and get away too.
Before Freddie and Mike Myres kill you.
Leave or stay to die, do it soon as Doomsday is coming too!

Joshua Bennett (14)
Hastingsbury Business & Enterprise College, Kempston

My Dream

Hello my reader, listen to something new,
I awoke this morning with a dream that will come true.
White and black on more than a chessboard,
A Muslim and Jew praying to the same lord.
A million men of every colour and race,
Gathering together all in one place.
A beautiful loving land,
Where all my brothers will walk hand in hand.
My plan, my goal, my dream, my soul.

After I awoke to this nightmare,
Where everyone is for themselves and don't seem to care,
I saw a man kill another for the shoes he wore,
A mother call her daughter a dirty whore.
A boy steals a car and ends up in jail,
Overdue mortgages coming in the mail.
A cat run over on the side of the road,
A dead child who ignored the Green Cross Code.
A tramp eating out of an old battered can,
And knives in the hands of young children.
If you help me I can help you and we'll make this dream come true.

Kyle Ford (14)
Hastingsbury Business & Enterprise College, Kempston

Great Flood

There once was a flood in town,
Everyone began to drown!
Loud screams let out,
Everyone wished for a drought.
That was the end of the town,
No more class clowns!

Wet, wet, wet,
All around,
The great flood of town.
Everyone screaming,
Reality not even close.

Molly Payne (15)
Hastingsbury Business & Enterprise College, Kempston

All Those Children

All those children starving without food,
Our parents getting in a mood
For not eating everything on our dish.
All those children want is a single wish.

All those children just want to die.
They think, *what's the point of living*, but why,
Why do we spend our millions on stuff we don't need
When kids out there are just desperate to feed.

All those children have nothing clean,
Why is the world being so mean?
They don't even have clean water.
How would you feel if that was *your* son or daughter?

All those children have a bare nothing,
No water no food, not a little something.
Their families consist of more than one or two,
But how would your family feel if that was you?

Katie Mayles (13)
Hastingsbury Business & Enterprise College, Kempston

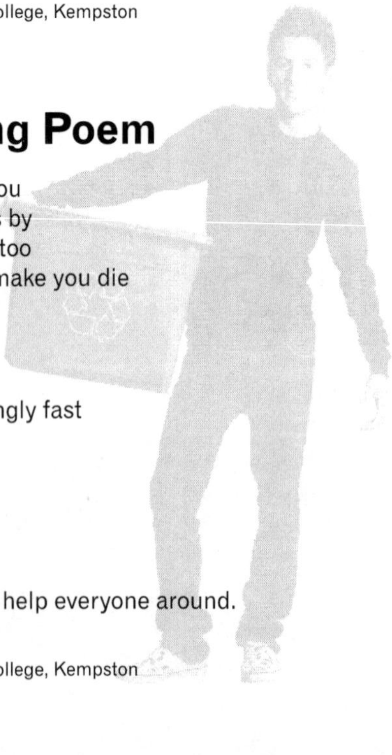

Acrostic Flooding Poem

B e aware of floods around you
E specially as the world goes by
W ater is nice but dangerous too
A n overflow of water could make you die
R each out to help
E veryone who is in a flood.

O ften
F looding can come surprisingly fast

F inding your house flooded
L ook around
O verflowing and
O verturned
D o you realise now?
S o dangerous is flooding so help everyone around.

Rhiannon Rickets (15)
Hastingsbury Business & Enterprise College, Kempston

The Morning Of The Flood

I did wake up one morning
My dream I had was good
But then I heard the shouted warning
Of the coming flood.

At this I sat bolt upright
My brother I did beat
To the window and the sight
Of water in the street.

I could not see the floor then
But standing in the flood
A man in a coat, a traffic warden
Knee deep in the mud.

I did not but just stand there
And a thought occurred to me
I would not be able to get there
The place called Hastingsbury.

Sam Briggs (15)
Hastingsbury Business & Enterprise College, Kempston

Who Are You?

Where are you when the sun don't shine,
Where were you when I said goodbye?
You say you're there but when I look
You're empty like a wordless book.
Remember us, remember you
Others in the world who go through it too.
Love is like war, like richness is poor
Love is secret, love is to share, love is to care.
But who can care when there's nobody there
When prayers are anonymous and calls are unanswered?
When love is to hate and hate is to love
When there is no one above who can help
Who can care, who is the answers to all my prayers?
You!

Serena Hannah Ruberto (13)
Hastingsbury Business & Enterprise College, Kempston

Save Our Power

Save the power,
Save the light,
Still no need
To say goodnight.

The sun is out,
Still shining bright,
So turn them off
And save the light.

The power is up
And it is strong.
How long is left
Till the power's gone?

Please be careful with our power,
Try to use it with care.
Be mindful every second, minute, hour.
Use it wisely not everywhere!

Sian Robinson (13)
Hastingsbury Business & Enterprise College, Kempston

Flood Sonnet

Your currents carry down sorry faces
Yearning out for forgiveness from your wrath
Tragedy in all near places
People's destinies take another path
You drown out people's cries
Destruction attaches itself to you like a tail
You care not about people's lives
As people sink their faces end blue and pale.
Families find themselves torn apart
People's belongings are exposed to all in the street
Everyone dreams for a fresh new start
Man's lifetime will forever feel incomplete
After you've gone the rebuilding begins
But in human eyes you will always win.

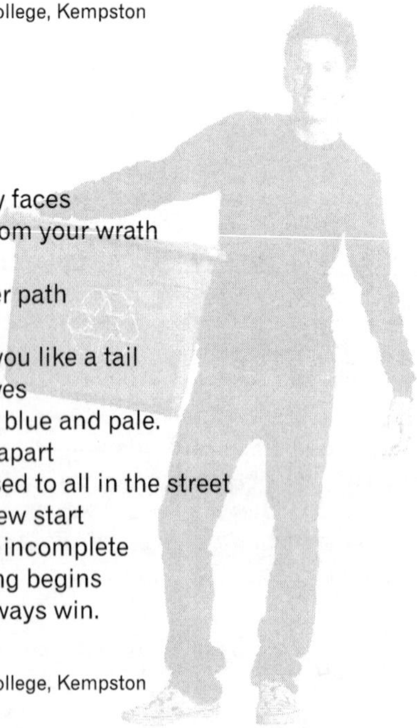

Ashley Field (16)
Hastingsbury Business & Enterprise College, Kempston

Water, Water

Sandbags
River banks
Floating cars
Rain in the rivers
Are making it hard.

Water, water everywhere
Grab your stuff
And run upstairs!

Dirty water
Muddy water
Chaos in the street

People just stand there
Soaked to their feet.
Water, water everywhere
Grab your stuff
And run upstairs!

Samantha Booth (15)
Hastingsbury Business & Enterprise College, Kempston

Flood

Floods are horrible, floods are bad,
Floods make you go mad.
Take your things, run upstairs and keep them safe
Here comes the fire engine, loud and clear
Coming to save us from the flood.
Rivers burst and let out water
They flood your house and get your things
Make sure they don't get your personal things.
Get your sandbags, don't be late
Else it will come gushing through your gate!
Put them in front of your door, not on the top floor.
When it ends the house is messy
But don't forget to wash the telly.

Rebecca Portman (13)
Hastingsbury Business & Enterprise College, Kempston

Graffiti

Over here
Over there
Graffiti is everywhere!

On a wall
In a school
Changes from big to small.

Purple, blue, pink or green
The things they write
Could be mean.

People come from
Far and near
To help the graffiti disappear.

Over here
Over there
Now graffiti is nowhere!

Gemma Martin (13)
Hastingsbury Business & Enterprise College, Kempston

Flood Poem

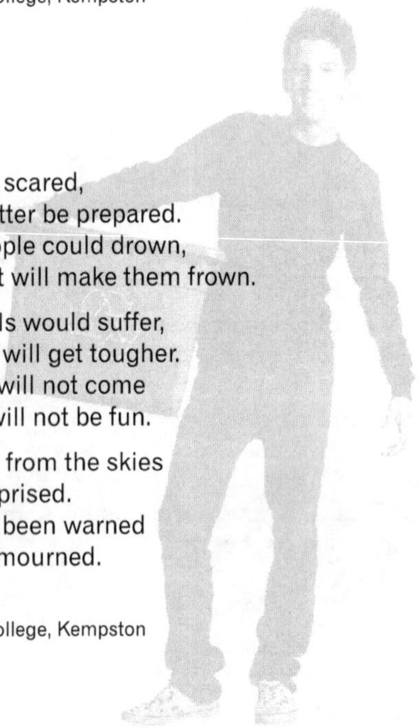

A flood is coming, everyone is scared,
A flood is coming, so you'd better be prepared.
A flood can be dangerous, people could drown,
Stuck in their houses, and that will make them frown.

Habitats would die and animals would suffer,
A flood is ongoing, conditions will get tougher.
The bible is fable; Noah's Ark will not come
We have to do it ourselves, it will not be fun.

Rain is severe, dropping down from the skies
Be prepared or you will be surprised.
A flood is coming, now you've been warned
Lives will end, people will get mourned.

David Roberts (16)
Hastingsbury Business & Enterprise College, Kempston

Flood Defence

F ree flowing
L ife risking
O verflowing Kempston
O h my goodness
D efend yourself, *quick!*

D on't go near it
E veryone needs rescuing
F lood is rising
E vacuate to your roof
N ow climb the ladder
C ome on, *quick!*
E veryone is safe now.

Charlie Thompson (14)
Hastingsbury Business & Enterprise College, Kempston

Flood In Kempston

There was a flood in town
That rapidly spread around
No one could see the ground
Rain was hurtling down
The only man who survived was a clown

The flood was going on for an hour
It was raining more than a shower
We ran out of power
I couldn't see a flower
After this shower it was our final hour
So say bye-bye to Kempston
And now I live in London.

Liam Joseph (14)
Hastingsbury Business & Enterprise College, Kempston

Environment

E xtinct animals and some endangered
N ature is being ruined
V ery bad pollution, noise, air and light
I gloos are being melted by global warming
R educe, reuse and recycle, save our planet
O zone layer is being destroyed
N atural disasters we cannot help
M ice are becoming homeless
E lephants endangered
N o, no, no, say no to this
T hink kind, think reduce, reuse and recycle.

Abigail Brooks (13)
Hastingsbury Business & Enterprise College, Kempston

A Poem On Flooding

I was woken one night by the thunder
Hmmm, why is my bed wet, I wondered.
When I stood up I had water to my feet
Looked out the window to see my car
Floating down the street.

I grabbed my jacket and got the umbrella out.
As I ran down the stairs, Mum began to shout,
'Get up, get up, get out the house!'
But Dad was in shock as quiet as a mouse.

Ajay Jhalli (14)
Hastingsbury Business & Enterprise College, Kempston

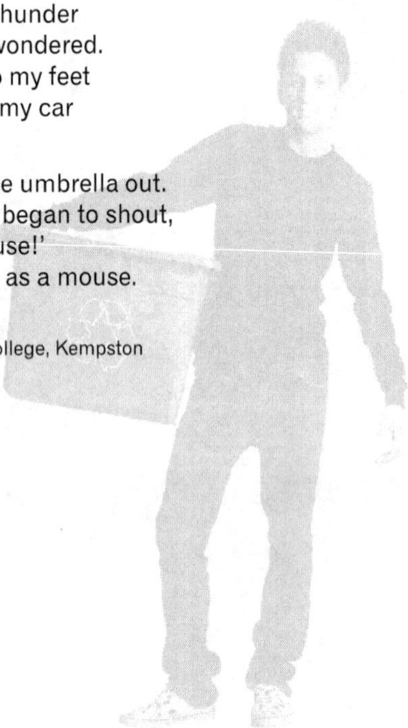

This World

Why is the world such a horrible place?
Is it because there is way too much waste?
Is it because no one recycles, not even a plastic yoghurt pot?
Is it because no one has any time?
But please just listen to this rhyme.
It's really not as hard as you think,
Just don't use too much water when filling your sink.
Recycle your pots, reuse your waste and this world won't
be such a horrible place.

Rebecca Bowers (13)
Hastingsbury Business & Enterprise College, Kempston

Flood

Get ready for the water
Get ready for the flood
It's coming with no warming
Coming with no luck

If you're not ready now
You don't have much hope
Get out the way
Out the way of the flood.

Gemma Swinscoe (15)
Hastingsbury Business & Enterprise College, Kempston

Rainbow

R ain started pouring until
A rainbow started forming and better still
I t seemed to be just in one place
N o one seemed to smile
B oats everywhere all of the while
O APs struggled around
W ater everywhere on the ground.

Maxine Stonebridge (14)
Hastingsbury Business & Enterprise College, Kempston

Flood

The rain is pouring down
Everyone in the town has a frown
Water is filling up in the street
People are losing their heat

A storm is forming in the sky
The weather women told me a lie
The teachers are starting to sigh
That's when I said goodbye.

Kirstie Roberts (15)
Hastingsbury Business & Enterprise College, Kempston

Flood Poem

The floods have come,
What can we do?
Protect your houses,
Don't let the floods affect you!

Put sandbags by your door,
Get your families out.
You need to get ready
For a bit of a drought.

Daniel Sherwood (14)
Hastingsbury Business & Enterprise College, Kempston

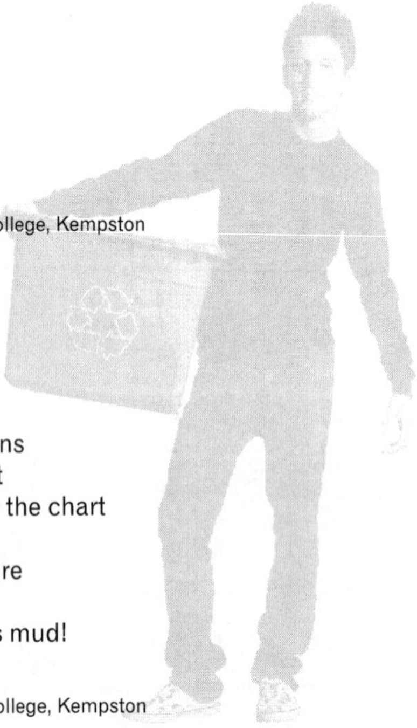

Flooding

F reezing water rushing in
L ots of water knocks over bins
O ver and over, lives fall apart
O h gosh, this rain level is off the chart
D own, down, the rain pours
I n this town you're never sure
N ever sure if it will flood
G ood old rain, look at all this mud!

Hannah Latton (13)
Hastingsbury Business & Enterprise College, Kempston

Untitled

Water crashes through doors
Stopping all the traffic
Floods rising with the rain
Isn't it just tragic?

Houses wrecked by the water
Barriers being put up to halt the flow
Not very nice is it eh?
Where will the water go?

Jonathan Bedford (15)
Hastingsbury Business & Enterprise College, Kempston

The Flood

Disastrous floods cause pain for many,
To help the villagers doesn't cost a penny.
Lots of houses are lost,
And being helpful does not cost.
Because a sad young man called Zak wishes his family back,
Now all he has to wear is his backpack!
Everybody gone, babies, sons, and my daughter.
Floating past me a young girl, I was close, almost caught her!

Leon Adjarkoh (13)
Hastingsbury Business & Enterprise College, Kempston

Be Good To The Planet

Why don't you go hiking
Then start recycling?
And don't go by car
Even if you're going far.
If you drop your litter
You should feel bitter.
Rainforests are dying
So let's stop flying.

Natasha White (13)
Hastingsbury Business & Enterprise College, Kempston

Flooding

F aster and faster the flood is coming
L ike a leopard through the trees
O ver the hill at the top of Kempston
O ver trees as it comes
D amaging homes and shops
I hear people yelling and screaming
N earer and nearer, coming closer
G ushing down the street, here it comes!

Charlotte Glover (13)
Hastingsbury Business & Enterprise College, Kempston

Flooding

F lowing rain is coming from the sky
L ittle of the sun is passing by
O ceans are filling deeper and deeper
O ther than the sun that's fading steeper
D ismal dull and rainy days
I s what's often coming our ways
N o more sun and bright skies
G one forever, so say your goodbyes.

Gemma Harry (14)
Hastingsbury Business & Enterprise College, Kempston

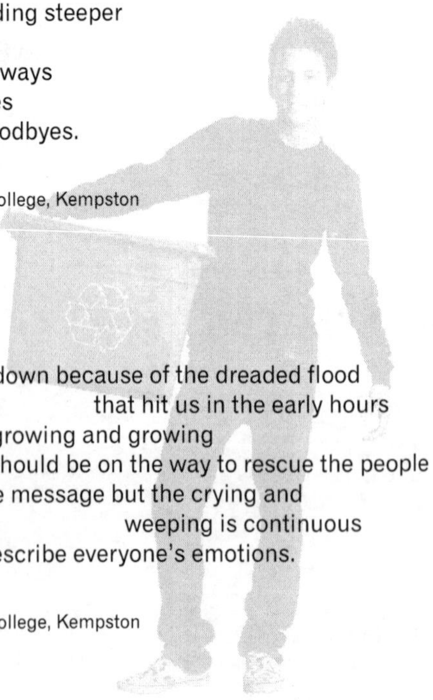

Flood

F eelings and emotions are down because of the dreaded flood
that hit us in the early hours
L oss of personal items are growing and growing
O n the way the firelighters should be on the way to rescue the people
O nwards and upwards is the message but the crying and
weeping is continuous
D evastated is the word to describe everyone's emotions.

Pavandeep Sangha (16)
Hastingsbury Business & Enterprise College, Kempston

Lights

L ights
I see them at home, at school, on the streets
G lowing bright day and night
H owever they aren't as bright as they seem
T hey're quickly absorbing our planet's energy
S o do your bit for the Earth today and switch them off!

Emily Paterson (13)
Hastingsbury Business & Enterprise College, Kempston

Litterbugs

L ove your planet
I nfecting your streets with all that mess
T ough if you can't be bothered to throw it away
T reat your planet fairly
E very time you litter you're hurting the planet
R ecycle, reduce, reuse.

Zhané Richardson-Downer (13)
Hastingsbury Business & Enterprise College, Kempston

Flooding Poem

F looding can cause lots of sadness
L ots of people going into madness
O thers are gone to go to pray
O h why can't this all go away?
D rowning people get very nippy, over there is a funky hippy.

Naomi Harvey (13)
Hastingsbury Business & Enterprise College, Kempston

Hell Then Hope

The *boom* of beastly bombs,
The creeping crack of pistols,
The open battlefield smells of gore
Which many claim they never saw.
The rapid rattle of rifles,
The ghostly repeated rat-ter-tat-er of machine guns.

The *thud* of long range artillery,
The whistle of flying shells,
The drone of bomber engines,
Then silence falls upon the battle.

An almighty *boom!*
Silence falls again,
The destroyer of worlds.

Men piled in mounds,
The ruby-red blood flows across the fields,
Silence.
Up pops hope!
A poppy.

Richard Spindley (13)
Northgate High School, Ipswich

My Ideal World

Don't need weapons
Don't need wars
To have a real good time.

So bring on peace
And bring on parties
Then we'll have a real good time.

Let's have all the same language
And all the same cash
Cures for all disease
And no more hash!

My perfect place
My ideal world
It's a world with appeal
It appeals to me, but what about you?

Hannah Meadows (12)
Northgate High School, Ipswich

Rainforests

All the beauty of rainforests in the world
All nature and plants
Animals and colour
But it has never stayed this quiet.

People started arriving
Trees started to disappear.
The trees stopped whistling in the wind.
The amazing animals started disappearing.

No hope for the future just in the past
Help was coming from far far away
To save the beauty and let it stay
Before it is stolen and taken away.

Keighley Andlaw (12)
Notley High School, Braintree

The Field

A calm morning,
No sound for miles.

Bang! Crackle!
A shot is fired!
A man falls to the ground,
A drop of blood drips onto the dry earth.

A child cries,
A woman screams,
Another shot is fired!
One more man falls dead to the ground.

No sound,
No movement,
Not even a whisper,
The battle is over.

A calm morning,
No sound for miles.

Sophie Buckley (12)
Notley High School, Braintree

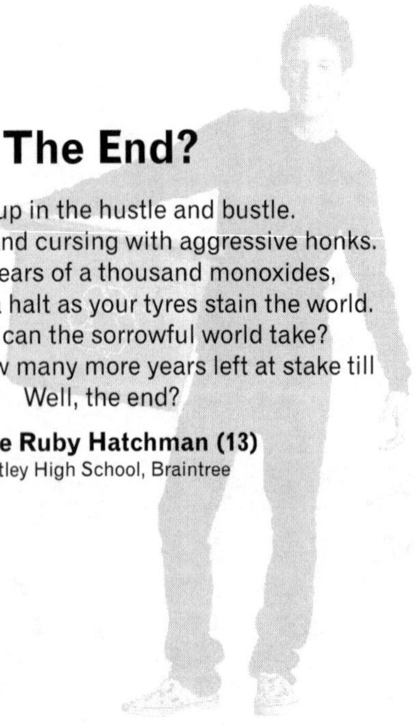

The End?

Caught up in the hustle and bustle.
Puffing fumes and cursing with aggressive honks.
Streaming tears of a thousand monoxides,
Screeching to a halt as your tyres stain the world.
How much can the sorrowful world take?
Who knows how many more years left at stake till
Well, the end?

Grace Ruby Hatchman (13)
Notley High School, Braintree

The Battlefield

The target is locked,
The shot is fired!
One more life is cut short,
The battlefield is like a graveyard.

The injured cry in pain.
No hope,
No help,
No happiness.

Finally the battle is over.
What was a field of death
Is now a field of beauty,
For what now lives there?

As red as blood,
As soft as silk.
What shows no fear
Hides the pain.

Louise Chappell (12)
Notley High School, Braintree

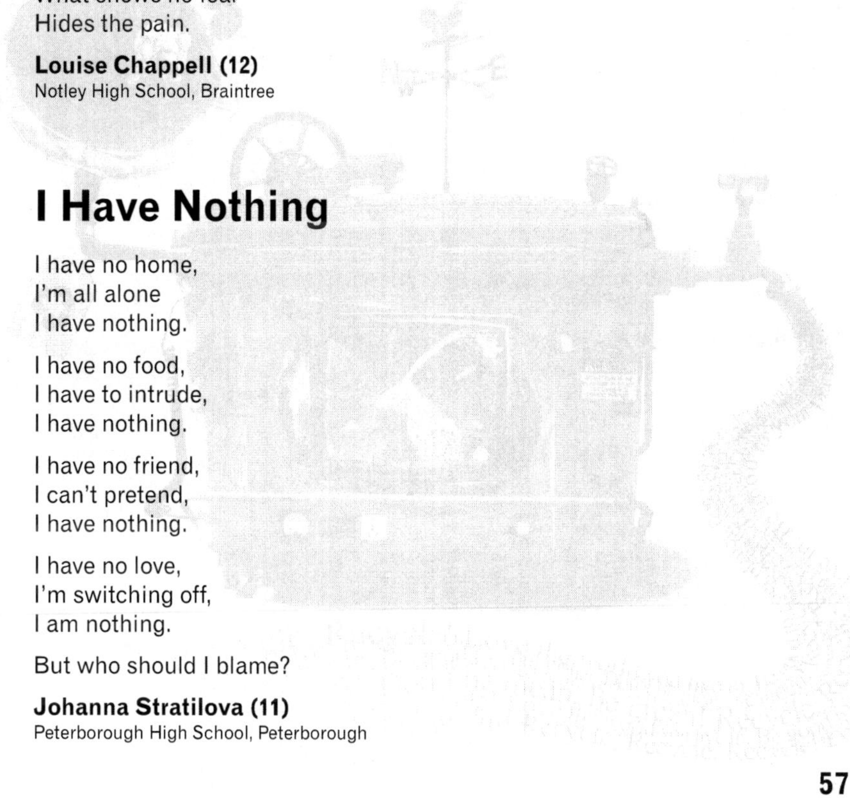

I Have Nothing

I have no home,
I'm all alone
I have nothing.

I have no food,
I have to intrude,
I have nothing.

I have no friend,
I can't pretend,
I have nothing.

I have no love,
I'm switching off,
I am nothing.

But who should I blame?

Johanna Stratilova (11)
Peterborough High School, Peterborough

War!

War is wrong,
War is bad,
War only makes people sad.

War can be spread
All over the news.
War can be read
But will give you the blues.

War is wrong,
War is sad,
War only make people mad.

War can mean dread
For all around.
War can mean dead
All over the ground.

War is wrong,
War is mad,
War only makes people bad.

War must be stopped
Before it is started.
War must be dropped
Before we are parted.

War is wrong,
War is sad,
War only makes people mad.

War is violence
Beyond compare.
People suffer in silence
Everywhere.

War is wrong,
War is bad,
War only makes people sad.

War must be banished
To our God we pray.
Before Mankind has vanished
For ever and a day.

War is wrong,
War is mad,
War only makes people bad.

War!

Amelia Rome (12)
Peterborough High School, Peterborough

Animals And Extinction

Why are they going?
What are we doing?

Polar bears were many
Now there's hardly any!
Dodos went before
Soon bears will be no more!
Where have they gone?
What have we done?

White Bengal tiger,
Types of rare spider
Missing from the landscape.
Now we're in a bad shape.
Where have they gone?
What have we done?

There are so many more
Protected by the law.
Although that is a fact
We still have to act.
Where have they gone?
What have we done?

Let's do what we can
And make a world plan
To find a global solution
Against mistreatment and pollution.
Then they won't be lost
And we won't need to count the cost.

Emily Ansell (11)
Peterborough High School, Peterborough

Where Are They?

The last time I came this way
Towering trees reached to the sky,
All around I could hear
The rustling sounds of fellow creatures.

But now I can see only
Pathetic stumps for miles.
All around I can hear
Nothing but deathly silence.

Where have they all gone
Those magical beasts
Who lurked here once
In an earthly paradise?

The two-legged Ones
Have done this thing
With iron monsters
Who obey their commands.

The trees I lived in
Are now furniture and firewood.
The animals are
Jackets and coats.

Perhaps the Ones will realise
What they have done
Before it is
Too late.

Their iron demons could
Plant trees back instead.
The hunting Ones could
Protect.

It wouldn't be long
Before the jungle took back its own.
But if they're going to do it
Where are they?

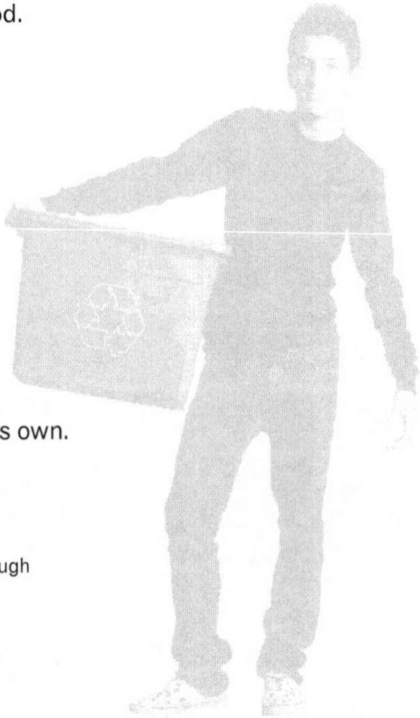

Niamh Khosla (11)
Peterborough High School, Peterborough

Am I Invisible?

Do you know what it feels like to be alone?
To come home to nothing
To be freezing
When nobody cares
There is nothing left to live for!

Do you know what it feels like to be left there starving
Not being fed, night after night?
There is no one to turn to
Except the darkness that is always there.
It is my only friend.

Do you know what it feels like to have the hope beaten out of you
Until the last bit's gone?
To feel so close
Yet so far.
Hope is the only strength.

Do you know what it feels like when there is no money left?
Finding leftover food,
Is the only way to survive.
Is there a way out
Or am I stuck here forever?

Why have you deserted me?
Should I be left like this?
Why can't I be like the other children?
Why doesn't anybody notice me,
Am I invisible?

Bethany Dillon (12)
Peterborough High School, Peterborough

Why Fight, Why Die?

Bullets, guns,
Mud, rain,
Mines, bombs,
Fighting, desperation,
Heroes, villains,
Innocent, dying,
These are ingredients of war.

There are some who think war is beauty,
They think to themselves, *war is good.*
But how can they think that?
The fighting, the despair, the dying.

Some people say, 'War is necessary
To keep the order in place.'
But why do they say that?
The heroes, the villains, the innocent.

And there are some who say, 'War is ugly,'
Who say, 'It makes me sick!'
But why do they say that?
The soldiers, the loyal, the hopeful.

I do not think war is good,
I do not think it is necessary,
But I do not think it is ugly.
Think of the brave soldiers
Laying down their lives for their beliefs.
I think some parts of war are noble and brave.

Kathryn Smyth (11)
Peterborough High School, Peterborough

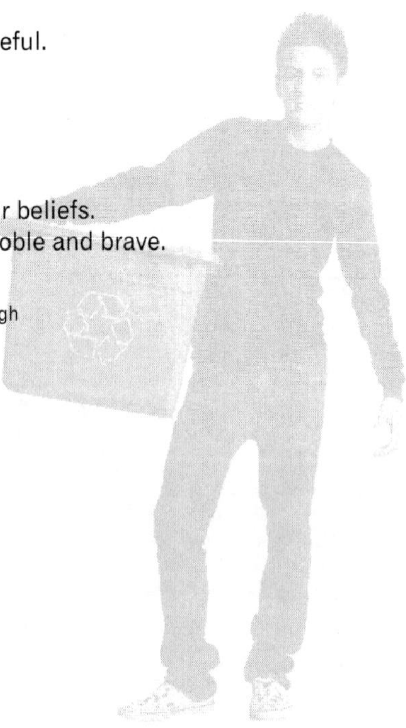

Animals

Extinction!
This is what the animals are facing
Birds, monkeys, beetles and more,
These are the animals of our rainforest.

Extinction!
This is what the animals are facing
Camels, snakes, lizards and more,
These are the animals of our desert.

Extinction!
This is what the animals are facing,
Penguins, seals, narwhals and more,
These are the animals of our polar countries.

Extinction!
This is what the animals are facing,
Foxes, bears, deer and more,
These are the animals of our forests.

Extinction!
This is what the animals are facing,
Lions, antelope, elephants and more,
These are the animals of our savannah.

Extinction!
Think of a world where no one fears
Fun, exciting, interesting and much more,
So give a shout, save the animals.

Abigail Foster (11)
Peterborough High School, Peterborough

The Big Green Litter Machine

L eaving litter lying around is for losers
I gnorance is litter and untidiness
T each children to pick up litter
T idiness is good
E veryone should know to pick up litter
R emember to prevent litter even reaching the floor.

Phoebe Benson (11)
Peterborough High School, Peterborough

Big Green Poetry Machine

Litter, litter on the floor
May harm animals much, much more.
People don't know what they are doing wrong
So make all of your litter and trash be gone!

If you have a sweet wrapper in the street,
Why not give the litter bin a treat.
They'll eat anything you don't need
Even if it is swede.

Treading on chewing gum is not pleasant
Neither is it for pheasants.
It is sticky on the ground
And people clear it up by the pound.

Apple cores on the grass
Go brown and mouldy when they hit the floor fast.
Wasps get them if they don't go in the bin
And then they start to smell and go thin.

Litter, litter on the floor,
Will harm animals much, much more.
People now know what they re doing wrong
So make *all* of your litter and trash be gone!

Freya Harvey (11)
Peterborough High School, Peterborough

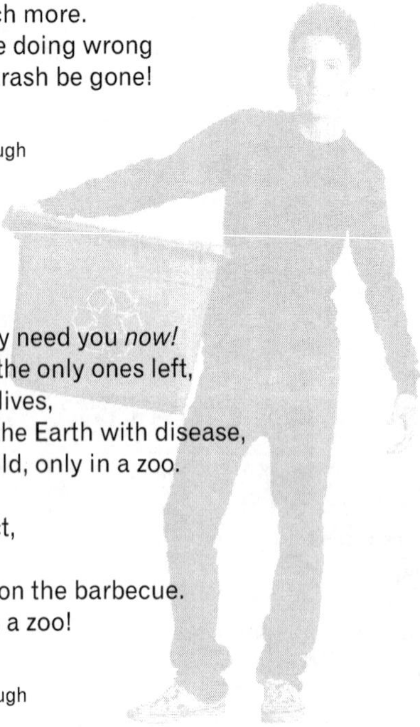

Extinction

E lephants are dying out they need you *now!*
X erox animals will soon be the only ones left,
T igers are losing their nine lives,
I nsects are overwhelming the Earth with disease,
N othing will be left in the wild, only in a zoo.
C himpanzees are very rare,
T asmanian tigers are extinct,
I guanas are disappearing,
O striches are getting eaten on the barbecue.
N one left in the wild, only in a zoo!

Imogen Pope (11)
Peterborough High School, Peterborough

War

The blood on the ground
Blazes like a fire,
The screaming gunshots
Cry out like a choir.
Nineteen-year-old boys risk their lives
For another person's battle,
But they have to fight
And hear the missiles rattle.
But now everything is still
Except the whisper of Death,
For on these grounds there is not one soul
And not one breath.
All those wasted lives
And wasted years,
Many a heartbroken family
And many shed tears.
But what is its purpose
What is it for?
It's just the stupidity of one man
That created a life-wasting war!

Rachel Senior (11)
Peterborough High School, Peterborough

Pollution

P is for pollution which is killing the Earth
O is for oxygen which we need to breathe
L is for land; don't dump waste in the ground
L is for love, we need to care for our planet
U is for unacceptable, we must stop polluting *now!*
T is for trouble, polluting will kill us all
I is for illegal, dumping waste in our seas
O is for our ozone layer being eaten away
N is for now, let's act before it is too late.

So let's all be good to our planet,
Make the world a better place to live
By doing our bit in protecting our environment.

Charlotte Hayes (11)
Peterborough High School, Peterborough

We Can Save Our Planet

Pollution here,
Pollution there,
Pollution everywhere.
Polluting does not help.
Here are ways
To make you switch and save.

Using cars is not good
It puts bad gases in the air so care.
Can we save the planet?
By using public transport or walking
We *can* save our planet.

Using computers is not good
It causes sound pollution so care.
Can we save the planet?
By using the computer for what you need
We *can* save our planet.

Reema Butt (11)
Peterborough High School, Peterborough

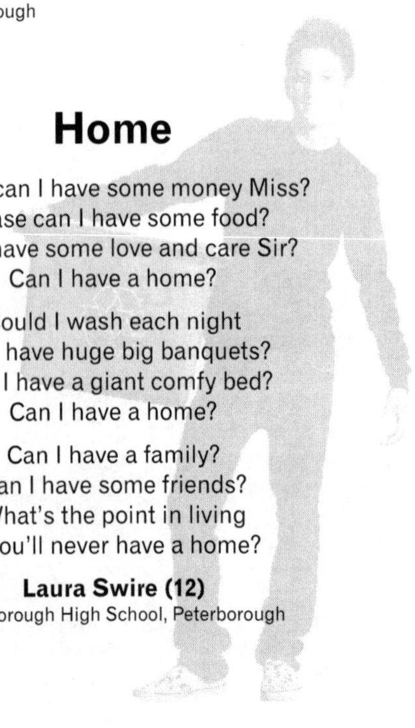

Home

Please can I have some money Miss?
Please can I have some food?
Can I have some love and care Sir?
Can I have a home?

Could I wash each night
And have huge big banquets?
Can I have a giant comfy bed?
Can I have a home?

Can I have a family?
Can I have some friends?
What's the point in living
If you'll never have a home?

Laura Swire (12)
Peterborough High School, Peterborough

Litter

Litter in the streets,
Litter in the park and fields,
Litter in the school.

Wherever it is,
Pick it up, it helps the Earth
And creatures on it.

These creatures are good,
They can't possible all go
Because of litter.

If they do, the world
Will become a boring place
With no excitement.

So for the sake of
The Earth, please pick up litter,
It makes a difference.

Emma Gibbons (12)
Peterborough High School, Peterborough

Save The Planet

Too many cars spilling out fumes
Destroying the ozone and causing monsoons
People are crying
Animals are dying

Too many factories polluting the atmosphere
Rivers are dirty they used to be clear
People are sighing
Fish are dying

The planet is overcrowded so rainforests are chopped
It's time this devastation stopped
The world is decaying
We need to stop delaying!

Abi Slater (11)
Peterborough High School, Peterborough

Pollution

All the animals are dying now,
Fish, bird and deer,
They have no place to sleep,
We have to save them!

The tree is dead now,
Oldest tree, youngest tree,
All are dying!
We have to save them!

The people are sick,
From air pollution, noise pollution.
Many people dying or sick,
We have to save them!

The Earth is dying now,
Animals, trees and people are dying,
We have to save them!

Tiffany Ho (12)
Peterborough High School, Peterborough

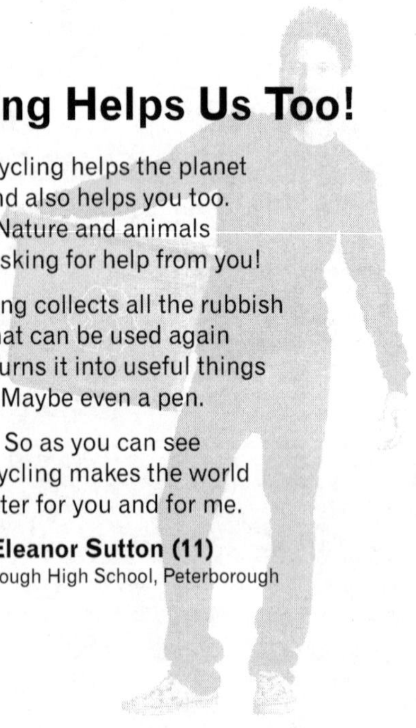

Recycling Helps Us Too!

Recycling helps the planet
And also helps you too.
Nature and animals
Are asking for help from you!

Recycling collects all the rubbish
That can be used again
And turns it into useful things
Maybe even a pen.

So as you can see
Recycling makes the world
Better for you and for me.

Eleanor Sutton (11)
Peterborough High School, Peterborough

Rainforest

R ainforests are places of natural beauty
A nimals live there
I n rainforests there are animals
N ature is what makes the rainforests what they are
F oxes and rabbits are some of the animals that don't live in the rainforests
O verall, rainforest are dying because we are killing them
R eptiles live in rainforests because of all the freshness
E xciting
S etting fire to the rainforests is how we are killing the rainforest
T igers live in rainforests.

Francesca Saberton (12)
Peterborough High School, Peterborough

Raging Rainforests

Cutting down trees
Green, brown and tall
God's creation pulled to the ground.

Forest fires
All blazing red and hot
Burnt to a crisp
Everything destroyed
Animals' homes recklessly ruined.
Destroyed without a care in the world.

Holly Lawler (12)
Peterborough High School, Peterborough

Don't You Litter

Don't you litter, it makes you bitter,
Why not put it in the bin?
Don't you litter, it makes you bitter,
Help us make the world clean.
It saves the animals, the birds and the bees
And not forgetting the trees.
So don't you litter, it makes you bitter
And save the world
For you and me!

Megan Watson (11)
Peterborough High School, Peterborough

Pollution

P ollution is ruining our world that is why I am going green
O ur ozone layer is getting smaller and smaller
L ook around and all you can see are factories smoking
L itter and pollution all around
U nderneath and on top
T he world is coming to an end because of it
I myself am trying to stop by going green
O ur world getting bigger and bigger due to pollution
N ow you can help the world by going green.

Ashna Avda (12)
Peterborough High School, Peterborough

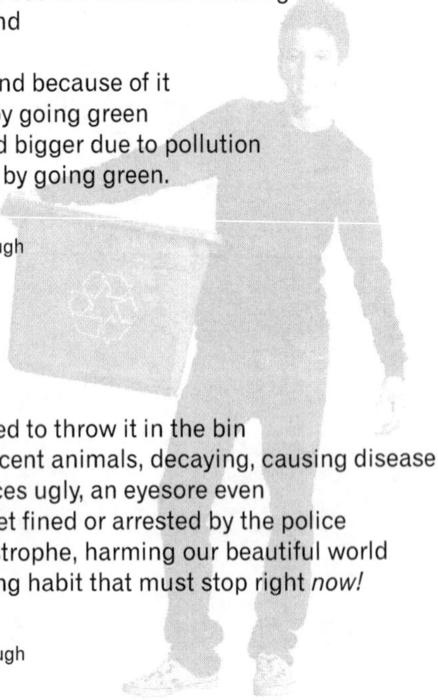

Litter

L is for lazy, can't be bothered to throw it in the bin
I is for injury, harming innocent animals, decaying, causing disease
T is for terrible, making places ugly, an eyesore even
T is for trouble; you could get fined or arrested by the police
E is for environmental catastrophe, harming our beautiful world
R is for revolting, a disgusting habit that must stop right *now!*

Rebekah Baugh (12)
Peterborough High School, Peterborough

Big Green

B eware to go green,
I t can help pollution, rainforests, recycling and more.
G o green to save the planet!

G o green to stop people littering, war, racism and extinction.
R emember to reduce cruel things happening, go green!
E asy job to go green,
E xtremely evil to increase extinction, global warming and more.
N ever stop to go green!

Nicola Wan (11)
Peterborough High School, Peterborough

A Poem

L itter louts throw down their rubbish
I n the bins please not on the floor.
T ins wash and place in the bin
T ake note the planet is being destroyed
E arth must breathe, don't suffocate it
R emember to recycle please.

Hollie King (11)
Peterborough High School, Peterborough

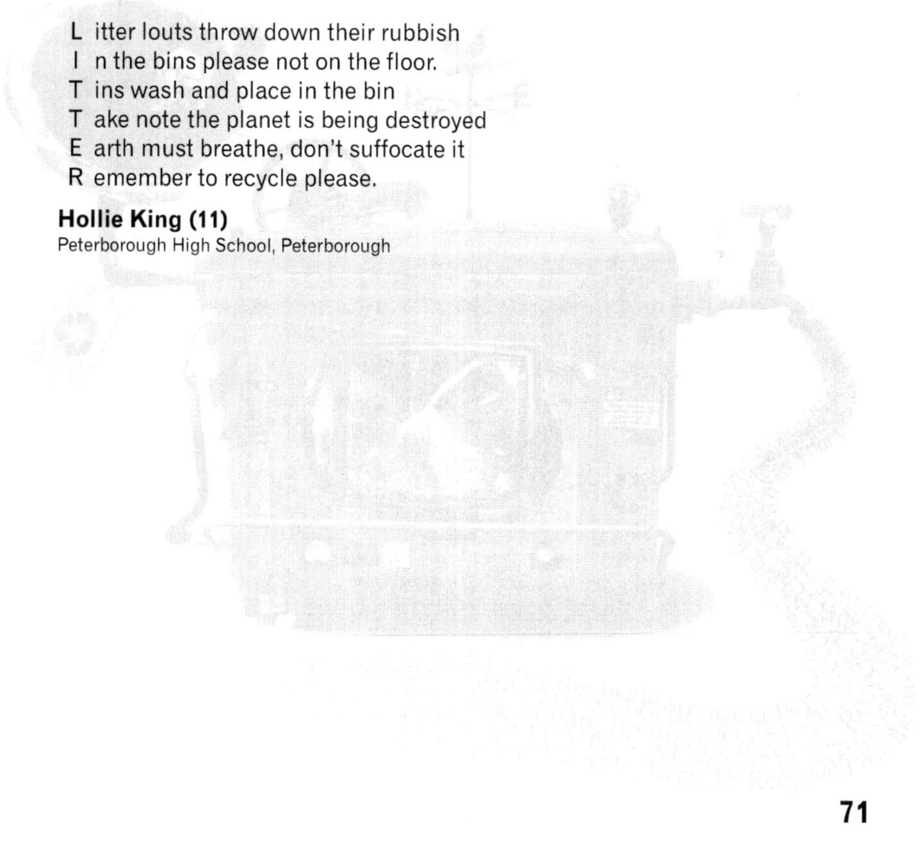

Environments

R educe reuse recycle are three ways we can help the environment
E nvironments are beautiful things made by God so let's not ruin them
D o your part to make the environment a safe place by using the three Rs
U se Earth's natural resources very wisely
C ans can be recycled along with cardboard and paper
E veryone can reduce the amount of trees being cut down by using less paper

R euse paper if you can by doing so you will be saving the amount of trees being cut
E veryone in a way can help the environment
U se cans paper and much more materials to make objects instead of wasting them
S ome people think it is funny to waste paper and I say it's not
E veryone who cares about the environment should try to convince their friends to care as well

R ecycle objects or materials that you do not need
E nvironment is a beautiful thing let's not ruin it
C an you use these three Rs
Y ou can make a difference in the world even if you're a kid
C an you then make a difference think about it
L ovely is a word to describe the environment let's try our best to keep that way
E lders at home might recycle tell them to encourage their friends to as well.

Ibara Razaq (12)
Putteridge High School, Luton

Our Planet

We are killing our planet
And if we don't stop soon,
The Earth will be silent
And there will be no moon.
Everything is dying.
The animals will be no more.
There will be no friendly neighbour,
Coming to knock upon your door.
The colours will be lifeless,
Black, brown and grey,
Surely we do not want our home
To end up this way.

And so we must take action,
Fight against ourselves.
So that eventually once more,
Joy will be brimming on dusty shelves.
We are in trouble now,
Mother Nature is calling
And if we do not answer,
Common decency will be falling.
The pollution is choking our planet.
We must provide it with clean air,
For if we do not help,
It will all end in despair.

Earth is crying for help.
We have caused all this trouble,
So now we must fix it,
By bursting our destructive bubble.

Imogen Wilson (12)
Robert Bloomfield Middle School, Shefford

There Was A Time . . .

There was a time when seas were blue
And the Earth was dressed in green
Along came technology
Colour was nowhere to be seen.

There was a time when forests were huge
And full of blooming trees
Along came paper factories
Trees were ripped to seams.

There was a time when snow was white
Skies were always blue
People used the gas lamps
To see me and you.

There was a time when sun shone down
Over our brilliant world.
Whatever happened to the shiny fish
Who swam by rocks and pearls?

So help us turn the world back
To the way you know it should
Even if you don't want to
Losing it wouldn't be good!

Sophie Risbridger (11)
Robert Bloomfield Middle School, Shefford

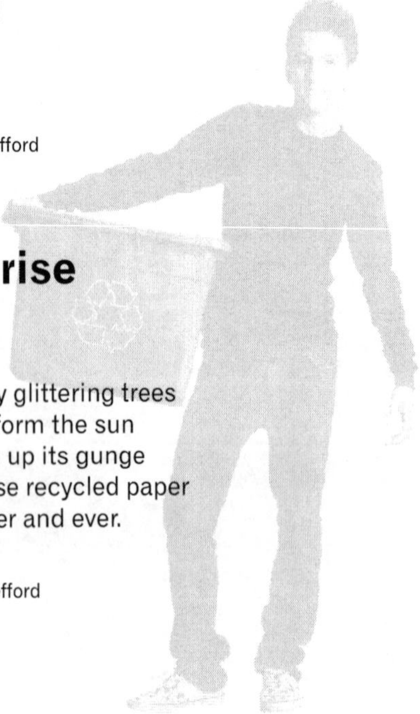

Rainforest Surprise

Exotically pretty
Warm sunshine breeze
Tropical rainforest with swishy glittering trees
Sticky hot weather gleaming form the sun
We'll help the rainforest clean up its gunge
We'll stop cutting trees and use recycled paper
Help save the rainforest forever and ever.

Basmah Malik (10)
Robert Bloomfield Middle School, Shefford

Earth's Feelings

On my way to school one day
I thought about the Earth
How it must be feeling
About what it is worth.

I think it might be annoyed
As it gave us country
And we give back wasteland
And cities and sewers.

I think it might be angry
As we've trashed its wonders
Littered them with rubbish
Making them look nasty.

I think it might be very sad
As it's being destroyed
It must feel terrible
Of letting mankind dwell.

Ben Lawrence (10)
Robert Bloomfield Middle School, Shefford

Dearest Mother Earth

Oh my dearest Mother Earth
We have done so much wrong
It seems Mother Nature hasn't won
With all your polluted seas.
Our father moon has disappeared
Some things we know cannot be changed.
The trees,
The seas,
The ice,
Our precious animals.
You've changed so much from what you were
No more blue skies or sweet green grass.
We're sorry we let you down
We know it's gone, it won't come back
From the people of your world.

Isobel Lowings (10)
Robert Bloomfield Middle School, Shefford

From My Window Perch

From my window perch I could see
The world was crisp and new
With all the brilliant colours
Green, yellow and blue.
But now it's gone; now it's changed,
What will we do?

From my window perch, oh how it's changed
Now I am old and so is Earth.
My tail and whiskers twitch.
The sky so grey, the land so brown,
Whatever was the glitch?
Crisp packets fly, gum sticks,
As I pad about the streets
Where has it gone, my safe haven, an old cat's itch.

Lottie Ashley (11)
Robert Bloomfield Middle School, Shefford

The Earth

As changeable as can be from raging hot deserts to the ice-cold Polar caps.
Life can be tough but that's no reason to disrespect the planet.
It gives us life and we give it pollution, it gives us love and we give it hate.

The planet is beautiful but tough, life is tough but we want it easy.
So we spoil it and don't listen to its pleas.
We kill its gorgeous animals for no reason and kill our own kind too.
We are the most hated species on Earth, that's our fault.

Nature is beautiful, from raging rivers to gushing geysers.
Nature is wonderful, from super snow to awesome autumns.
Nature is brilliant but we spoilt it,
We kill it for metal gadgets, that's wrong, stop it *now!*

Bethany Summerfield (13)
Robert Bloomfield Middle School, Shefford

Do You Think The Earth Wants This?

Do you think the Earth wants this?
The seas filled with oil barrels
And rivers full of dying fish.

Instead of looking after our trees
We chop them down
Making room for more factories.

The forests supply everything we need
Nuts, berries and wild boar
All this destroyed by Man's evil greed.

What are we polluting this Earth For?
When we all know
It can't take it anymore?

William Martin Wren (10)
Robert Bloomfield Middle School, Shefford

Carbon Footprint

The energy is running out,
We have no coal or fuel,
We need to save our planet
So we need to make a rule.
Day by day, year by year,
Carbon footprints are bigger,
Still no one is in fear.
Our rule to save our planet is
Save water, it's a must,
Turn off lights, turn off TVs,
Make sure you save the elephant's tusks.
The animals are endangered
With poachers hunting them down,
Some are caught in big bad traps
And some are left to drown.
With all these environment issues,
You cannot start to help
Because our planet is collapsing
So go out and help!

Laura Gleave (12)
Sheredes Secondary School, Hoddesdon

The Anteater

Shuffling through the undergrowth,
Sniffing around holes,
Searching for some food,
To suck up his nose.

Eating ants rapidly,
The anteater comes,
Dashing through the forest,
The anteater runs.

Stomping his feet loudly,
Searching out his food,
His long sticky tongue
Got him in lots of fun.

Eating ants rapidly,
The anteater comes,
Dashing through the forest,
The anteater runs.

With the poachers coming
Hunting him out,
The anteater runs,
Sniffing with his snout.

Eating ants rapidly,
The anteater comes,
Dashing through the forest,
The anteater runs.

With guns at the ready,
They take aim and fire,
The anteater is no more.

Eating ants rapidly,
The anteater comes,
Dashing through the forest,
The anteater runs.

Left to just lie there,
And wither away,
The anteater will not come out today.

Emily Sargent (12)
Sheredes Secondary School, Hoddesdon

Animals And The Sea

The horse galloped across the sandy beach
Rapidly waves splashing at their feet
Children playing volleyball
Having a picnic after all
The rider bouncing all over the place
People saying what a disgrace
Children giggling
Babies wiggling
People munching
Whilst crunching
Horse neighing
Nan and Grandad lying
Seas turning green
Kids looking mean
Oh no!

What are we going to do?
Some need to go to the loo
No toilet to be seen
People not looking clean
Palm trees being cut down
Animals are falling
Leaves are blowing into town
On a Sunday morning
People dumping waste in the sea
Fishes are getting hurt
Sir had lost the lighthouse key
Keep your eyes alert
Dolphins are diving out of the ocean
Children looking amazed
Parents covering kids in sun lotion
Whilst the temperature raised.

Rebecca Harvey (12)
Sheredes Secondary School, Hoddesdon

Don't You Care?

There are animals out there
Don't you care?
That's their home you're ruining
That's not fair

What happened to recycling?
Don't you care?
You could really help
That's not fair.

Trees cutting, stop it now!
Don't you care?
Carbon dioxide is in there
That's not fair.

Seas and oceans should be clear
Don't you care?
Not full of litter as soon as you get near
That's not fair.

Animals' cruelty
Don't you care?
They are something too
That's not fair.

Stop it all it's not right
Save the world
No need to fight.

Brooke Leigh Mitchell (12)
Sheredes Secondary School, Hoddesdon

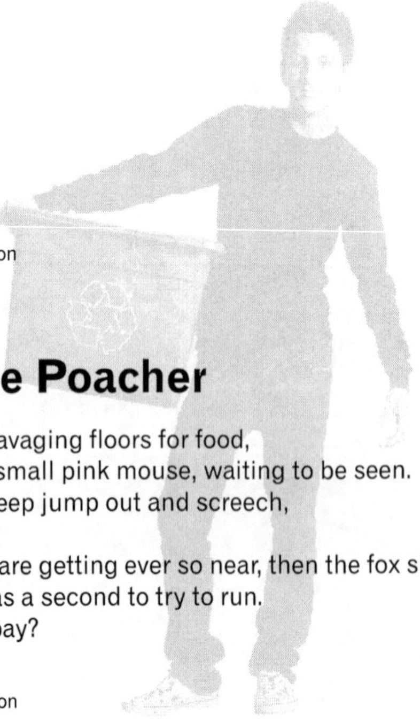

The Fox And The Poacher

Rustling through the leaves, savaging floors for food,
Hungry then suddenly sees a small pink mouse, waiting to be seen.
The men in the camouflaged jeep jump out and screech,
They leap with their shotguns.
The fox is transfixed, the men are getting ever so near, then the fox shows fear.
Bang! Goes the gun, the fox has a second to try to run.
Does he get away or does he pay?

Jade Summeer Carrig (11)
Sheredes Secondary School, Hoddesdon

Being Green Poem

Cutting down trees
Kills all the bees.
Habitat destruction
Causes home eruption.
Pollution needs reducing
Less packaging needs producing.
So get involved
And the problem's solved.
Do not ignore
The knock at the door
Fill your charity sacks
With lots of knick-knacks.
It will help in the long run
To make our world more fun.
So do not dismiss
The importance of this
For what happens today
Will not go away.
It affects us all
So don't be a fool
Recycle today
To make it go away.
Think of our future, make it greener
Spread the word to keep it cleaner!

Sarah Cole (12)
Sheredes Secondary School, Hoddesdon

Litter, Litter On The Ground

Litter, litter on the ground,
Animals die,
We all wonder why.
Don't be bitter, you know it's your litter!

We can all help,
Cut down going to a shop,
Unless you're wise and put your litter in a bin,
Because this thing has got to stop.

Demi Mitchell (12)
Sheredes Secondary School, Hoddesdon

The Ice Caps

This world is heating like an oven,
The ice caps are melting,
People running and screaming
But this is just the beginning.

Buildings crumbling to the ground,
Flattening people and making them drown.
All the people can do is nothing
Because the water is slowly rising.

The whole world is now in danger
Because it is winter.
The survivors from the flood were lucky,
Until the water froze and froze them badly.

You could see people's faces stuck in the ice
Like they were screaming in pain.
They looked like they were stuck there
Turning into fossils only as white as the light.

Summer came soon and the ice started to melt,
This caused the flood to start again.
These are the dark times now
As the age of ice and water began.

Jack Ryan Hardy (11)
Sheredes Secondary School, Hoddesdon

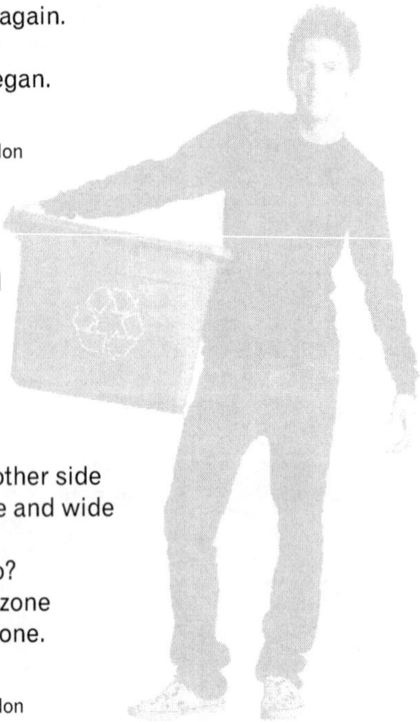

My Green Poem

I look out the window to see
The luscious green grass
I see the tractor all
Painted shiny and brass

I look out the window on the other side
I see the motorway all horrible and wide
Why do the cars go so slow?
Why can't the light just say go?
All the fumes going into the ozone
I wish there was one car all alone.

Charlie Rooney (13)
Sheredes Secondary School, Hoddesdon

The Planet

The world is not fair
Our planet is dying
But no one seems to care.

People would rather put hairspray on their hair
Our planet is dying
But no one seems to care.

Driving around in big fast cars going nowhere
Our planet is dying
But no one seems to care.

Cutting down trees that help to produce our air
Our planet is dying
But no one seems to care.

This is too much to bear
Our planet is dying
But no one seems to care.

Our planet is dying
But no one seems to care.

Demi Sorrell (12)
Sheredes Secondary School, Hoddesdon

Melting Ice Caps

Slowly, slowly the ice began to melt
Icebergs shrink and they begin to sink
The polar bears are homeless
The penguins have no sleep
The water level rising
The world is going to sink
Our homes will all be flooded, the roads and fields too
Food will be a shortage, most lives will be taken
Shortages will be taken to the extreme
Will it ever stop?
Help global warming by turning off what's not in use
There really is no excuse, not to be green, it's not obscene
Animals becoming extinct, in the floods we shall sink!

Britney Pettifer (11)
Sheredes Secondary School, Hoddesdon

We're Killing Our Planet Again

We're running out of oxygen
The trees are falling down
The animals are homeless
The wood is sent to town.

The wood is turned to paper
The paper is thrown away
Paper is taken to the countryside
And left to decay.

Recycling, recycling, recycle today
If you don't recycle, expect to pay!
Glass, plastic and bottles are also recyclable
So pop down to your local recycling point
And throw them away.

Please recycle
It will do us good
We hope you all understand
Recycle, recycle, recycle!

Jodie Freestone (13)
Sheredes Secondary School, Hoddesdon

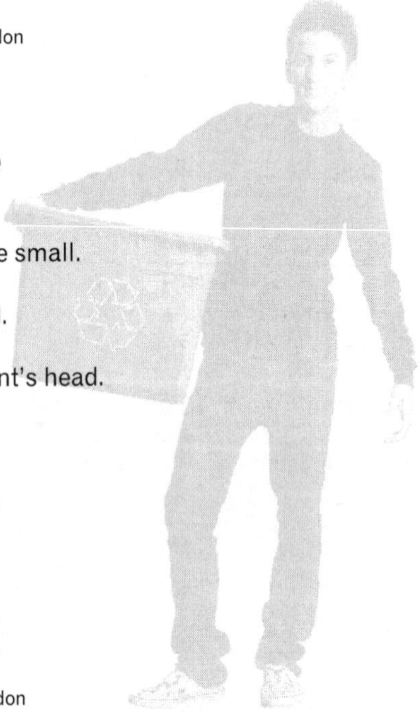

Big Green Issue

They're fat and tall,
People who kill them are quite small.
They rush through the land
And get stuck in sinking sand.
Bang! Bang! They're dead,
They can now rest the elephant's head.
When you drive your car
You pollute the sky.
This ain't no lie,
Closer and closer till you die.
The sea is blue,
If you pollute it turns to goo.
Don't pollute the air
Or you will deal with me!

James Lovelock (12)
Sheredes Secondary School, Hoddesdon

The Big Brown Bear

The brown bear climbed the tree
I think it just wanted to be free
The fireman came to rescue her
But found there was too much fur.

The bear could not get down
Then came a clown
To cheer her up
Whilst the firemen cuddle a pup.

Its baby cub
Drank some water out of a tub
The mother started crying
Desperately trying
To get out of the tree.

A few days later
In came a gator
The bear fell off
Then he gave a cough.

Danielle Kersey (12)
Sheredes Secondary School, Hoddesdon

Monkeys In The Rainforest

As the monkey swings from tree to tree eating his banana,
Jumping through branches, rustling all the leaves,
Finding something good to eat to fill his fat tummy,
Watching other monkeys hugging their little friends,
Wishing he was one of them but no one does care.
He dreams about a family then wakes up in the morning
But knows it's just a dream.
He sees all the girls but not one of them is free.
But then that day he sees the one coming to his need,
He runs to her looking in her eyes, he holds her tight, not letting go.
She kisses him on the cheek; hand in hand they climb the tree.
If the trees are cut down, all *will* disappear.
No monkeys, food or anything, just broken stumps and fear.

Jasmine Robinson & Jodie Field (12)
Sheredes Secondary School, Hoddesdon

Animal Cruelty

What have I done?
We used to have fun
Now they don't want me
All I have left is this flea
We used to have good times together
Any weather
But now I'm on my own
It's a shame I don't have a clone

They promised me forever
Perhaps I'm not that clever
To understand the human mind
I must be blind
Not to see what was going to happen

I need a home
Or maybe a bone
Streets is where no dog should be
This animal cruelty shouldn't happen to animals like me!

Rebecca Leach (12)
Sheredes Secondary School, Hoddesdon

The Planet

Roses are red,
Violets are blue,
There is a hole in the ozone layer too!

Turn off the taps,
Shut all the doors,
Make sure you recycle,
It will help you and me.

Save all the plants,
Donate some money,
It will save us forever and ever.

Save the forest,
Save the sea,
Saving all this will save you and me!

Aaron Murphy (11)
Sheredes Secondary School, Hoddesdon

Bad Day In The Rainforest

There is a big cat called Jim
He has to get some dinner
He doesn't know what to bring
Bad day in the rainforest

He tries to catch a deer
The deer flees
The deer brings fear
Bad day in the rainforest

The deer gets a mate
Its' time for dinner
'We'll be late.'
Bad day in the rainforest

Jim dies
Terrible death
On the floor he lies
Bad day in the rainforest!

Samuel Tabib (12)
Sheredes Secondary School, Hoddesdon

Make It Fair!

Animal habitat destruction and cruelty,
Stupid people dumping rubbish in the seas,
Icebergs melting everywhere,
People cutting down trees without a care.
Oil been spilled on the land,
All these nasty things should be banned.
So when the ice has melted
And the seas begin to rise,
It will show them naughty people with their own eyes
That we're destroying the world every night and day,
And in a few years we're *all* going to pay.
So take some notice because we all might die.
Why are people doing this, why, why, why?
So you're living in this world and you have got to give it care,
If everyone helps then it will make it fair.

Alfie Wise (12)
Sheredes Secondary School, Hoddesdon

Gone Off

If you eat McDonald's,
Don't throw it on the ground.
Throw it in the bin,
It could save you quite some pounds.

Litter is everywhere,
On the floor and on the trees.
If you don't throw it in the bin,
It could attract some bees.

Litter is messy,
It really is a disgrace,
So try to do your best
To save the human race.

Think about it.
In a couple of years
All the mess will go away,
And hear the people cheer.

Matthew Sheppard (11)
Sheredes Secondary School, Hoddesdon

R, R And R!

It was just last week I noticed the rubbish in my bin
Just how much was in there from paper and card to tin
The dustman will come along and empty all the bins
The clanging of the bottles rolling here and there
Some people just don't really care
They throw their rubbish in the street
Which in the wind can wind up round your feet
Recycling is the answer so let's remember to bin your rubbish every day
Keep your area cleaner and your grass will look greener
Glass bottles in the black recycling box, household rubbish in the purple bags
Paper and tin cans collected round the clock or landfills full in nine years
The answer? Recycle, reduce and reuse!

Bradley Hoskin (12)
Sheredes Secondary School, Hoddesdon

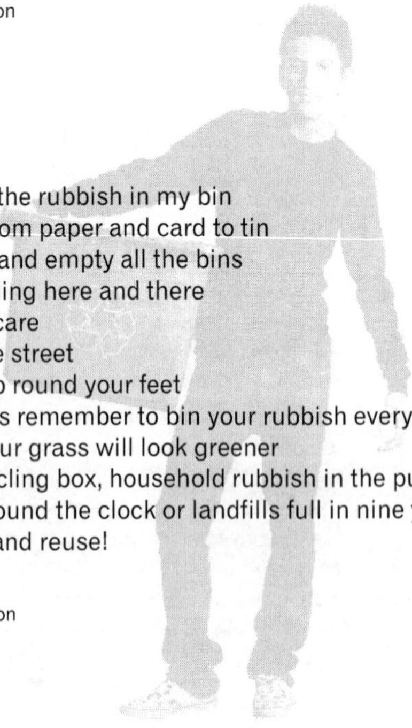

Skins And Paws

The jeep passes by
Their recent victims on the back
Victory shouts from the jeep
Care for the wildlife they lack

Once a peaceful place
Ravaged by hunters
Leaving for the markets
Stocked up on trophies and guns

They leave their mark
A forest full of death
Corpses scattered everywhere
Leaving not one animal left

A forest in tranquillity
Disrupted by war
Blood spilling
All for skins and furs.

Daniel Coss (12)
Sheredes Secondary School, Hoddesdon

The Big Polar Bear

The big polar bear was swimming through the sea
Looking for something every nice to eat.

White and fluffy, fat and chubby,
Friendly to you and me.

Icebergs melting, poachers lurking,
Not a wonderful place to stay.

With cold winter days and the cold winter nights,
Polar bears are all alone.

Crawling, crawling, yawning, yawning,
Poachers take their aim.

A shot to the head, don't care if he's dead,
They use his skin as a rug.

Aiden Bristow (12)
Sheredes Secondary School, Hoddesdon

Recycle The World

We need to save our planet
We need to do it now
If we don't the world will die
And if we do it we will fly.

We must recycle for cleanness
So the world doesn't have space for fearless
Let's do this and be green
And grow the apples to be seen.

Let's see a waterfall
Plus a down stream
It will be so clean
And then we will be seen.

So let's be persuasive
And give them what they want
So if we give it all
Then we don't have to moan and groan.

Billy Melton (12)
Sheredes Secondary School, Hoddesdon

Poaching

Leaping through the outback
Jumping at high speed
The kangaroo is running
Just to get a feed.

Brown and fluffy
Babies running alongside
Gunfire echoes off the land
The baby runs no more.

As they stuffed her body
The blood was red and squishy
As they chopped off her head
As if she was put to bed.

Katie Elliott (12)
Sheredes Secondary School, Hoddesdon

Energy Saving

The planet's running out of steam,
We're running out of fuel.
To help save the planet,
The planet needs you.

Turn off the switches,
Turn off the taps.
Don't forget to turn down
Your thermostat.

If you usually drive to school,
Next time don't take the car.
Walking is the easier option,
Plus your school can't be that far.

When you're not using it,
Turn off your TV
And remember once you've done this,
It will be safe for you and me.

Lily Wrighton (12)
Sheredes Secondary School, Hoddesdon

Poaching Pandas

Black and white panda bear
Sitting in the trees
Thinking nobody was there
How I wish he could have fled
A weapon is flung, it's a spear!
The panda falls down dead!
It hits him squarely on the head
Our animals they live in fear
Helpless pandas, they're no more
Black and white fur, a clawed paw
I ask you Sir, is this right?
Killing our animals, you have no right!

Lucy Dore (11)
Sheredes Secondary School, Hoddesdon

Rainforest

The tigers like a rainbow
Hides from every rain
The tiger comes out
Searching for its prey.

The parrot is a copycat
Learning new words
The only thing that stops him
He can't find the trees.

Oh woodpecker, oh woodpecker
Don't peck me
I'm gonna be chopped down
Go peck another tree.

What happened to the trees?
Where's the plane full of bees?
Weird things are happening
Oh please someone, help me.

Jimmy Jacobs (12)
Sheredes Secondary School, Hoddesdon

Snow Tiger

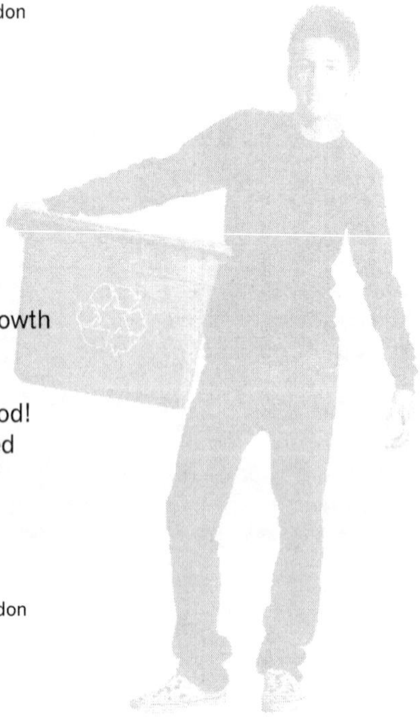

Running through the snow
As camouflaged as can be
Nobody can see him
Apart from me and you.
Stalking through the undergrowth
He searches for his food
You better run away
Because he's in a hungry mood!
These animals are endangered
Their fur is very nice
It might look good on you
But much better on the tiger.

Alby Santagata (11)
Sheredes Secondary School, Hoddesdon

Rainforests

Life is killed day by day
Trees are all cut down
Animals extinct every year
Just to build an ugly town.

Trees being cut down
Less oxygen in the air
No homes for birds to live
Still, nobody cares.

Poachers illegally hunting
Dirty water for fishes to swim
Animal parts sold for medicine
Why is our world so grim?

If only people recycled paper
And turned off lights after use
Then none of the world would be crying
Start to help as there is no good excuse.

Eleanor Pollock (12)
Sheredes Secondary School, Hoddesdon

The Chained Up Dog

I wish that I was told what I've done wrong
Why must I be chained up and left alone so very long
They seemed so glad to have me when I was growing up
There were so many things we'd do when I was just a pup
The master said he'd train me as a companion and a friend
The mistress said she'd never fear to be alone again
The children said they'd feed me and they did if I would only stay
But now the mater says 'No time'
The mistress says I weep
She doesn't want me in the house not even to be fed
The children said they'd walk me now they say not now
I wish I could tell them how I really feel.

Harleigh Fielder (13)
Sheredes Secondary School, Hoddesdon

Poaching

The mighty grey elephant
So proud, so big, so tall,
The poacher hiding in the trees
Then the mighty elephant falls.

The horrible ugly poachers
Shot the elephant dead!
The big grey elephant screamed
As they chopped off his head.

The poacher being big and bright
Making clothes and jewellery
They sent their bodies down to town
And he was happy in glory.

The herd of elephants were crying
As they watched them go to town.
Because their tears were soggy,
They all came tumbling down.

Charlotte Cusack (12)
Sheredes Secondary School, Hoddesdon

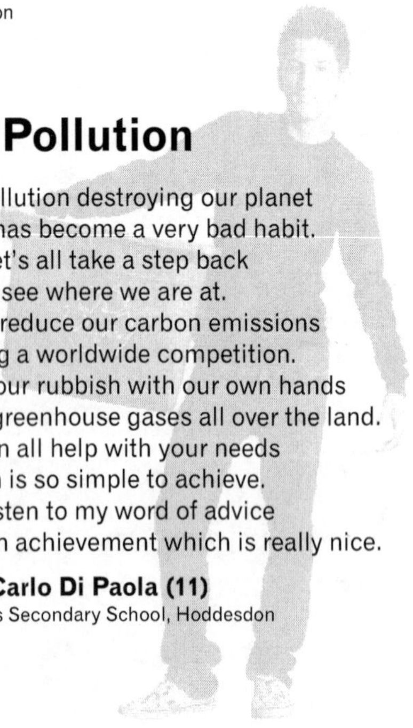

Pollution

Terrible pollution destroying our planet
Already it has become a very bad habit.
So let's all take a step back
To see where we are at.
Let's try to reduce our carbon emissions
By having a worldwide competition.
By recycling our rubbish with our own hands
Can reduce the greenhouse gases all over the land.
This can all help with your needs
Which is so simple to achieve.
Now listen to my word of advice
Being green is an achievement which is really nice.

Carlo Di Paola (11)
Sheredes Secondary School, Hoddesdon

We're Killing Our Planet Again

We're running out of oxygen
The trees are falling down
The animals are homeless
The wood is sent to town

The wood is turned to paper
The paper's thrown away
Paper's taken to the countryside
And left to decay

Recycling, recycling, recycle today
If you don't recycle expect to pay
Glass, plastic and bottles too
So pop down to your local recycling point and throw them away
Otherwise the world will pay

Please recycle, it will do us good
We hope you all understood
Recycle, recycle, recycle!

Chloe Verrier (12)
Sheredes Secondary School, Hoddesdon

Ice Caps Are Melting

People's homes will get washed away,
Old people have nowhere to stay.
All the crops and food will die,
People of the world will surely sigh.
All the ice caps are melting.
We want to see our grandchildren alive.
Also animals plant a beehive.
Parts of the world will surely end
If we don't come together, fix and mend.
Let's hop on a bus and take a trip,
Don't use so many cars, now that's a tip.

Chloe Allen (11)
Sheredes Secondary School, Hoddesdon

Save Trees

Trees are tall and thick
So why kill then in one little trick?
Abracadabra trees are gone
Gone, gone, in one little song.
Trees sway back and forth
But the size of thirty-thousand dwarfs
If it collapses you know you'll hear it
Thump on the ground, nice and loud!
Cutting trees does not help
When you can't hear them yelp.
Trees are lovely and soft
Better then the old Christmas tree in the loft.
Dusty and mostly rusty, trees nice and smooth
Better then my grandad's rotten old tooth.
Chainsaws are mean but no good to the green.
Trees help stop floods, they slow it down
Basically it's a king with its crown.

Edward Dent (12)
Sheredes Secondary School, Hoddesdon

Save The Planet

Roses are red
Violets are blue
Turn off the tap
It will help you!

Save the bath
Have a shower
Please don't have one
Every hour.

Read the paper
Recycle it please
Don't eat junk food
Eat some peas.

Global warming is hot
It could melt a robot.

Thomas Hurst (11)
Sheredes Secondary School, Hoddesdon

Endangered

Silently through the snow
Leopards hunt their prey
And do it their own way

Hunters come and go
Shooting bullets
So the leopards hide down low
Some will survive but you'll never know

They take their next shot
Leopards lying dead on the floor
So the hunters complete their plot
And as for the leopards they will never see their loved ones anymore

Blood and guts everywhere
People walk by and stop and stare
So if you ever walk there
You will need to be aware.

Miroslav Gospodinov (12)
Sheredes Secondary School, Hoddesdon

Do Your Bit!

Turn the lights off,
Take a shower,
People are wasting too much power.

Take your unwanted clothes
To the charity shop,
All this landfill just has to stop.

Stick all your green waste in the compost bin,
To put it anywhere else is truly a sin.
Mother Earth needs our help, there's so much to do,
Don't leave it to others, it all starts with you!

Katie Carmichael (11)
Sheredes Secondary School, Hoddesdon

Little Tiger Millie

Little white tiger Millie
Lives in the trees
She likes to eat bees.

Playing with her sisters
Dancing in the snow
Tiny tiger paw prints
Show the way to go.

Hunters on the go
Searching for a prize
It's too late they have to show
The hunters hunt but do they succeed?

Little white tiger Millie
Lying in the snow
Poor little Millie
The sisters attack to show.

Chloe Deering (12)
Sheredes Secondary School, Hoddesdon

Rainforest

R ising sun, rising temperature
A nimals picking fresh food from trees
I nsects crawling into pieces of bark
N ear and far noises from the forest
F rogs jumping from one lily pad to another
O range coloured flowers reflecting in the sun
R ain dripping off the skin
E verlasting rainfalls
S mooth animal skin rustling against leaves
T emperature cooling as nightfall descends.

Rosie Kermode (11)
Sheredes Secondary School, Hoddesdon

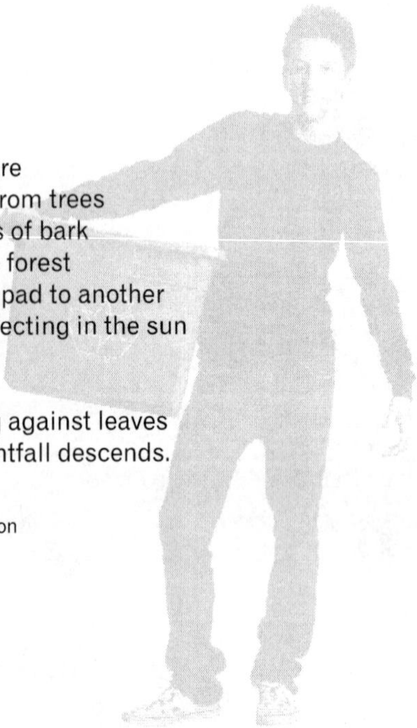

The Rhinos

Across the plains of Africa
The rhino herd do roam
Grazing on the grass lands
Of their green and pleasant home

Hiding in the bushes
The hunter points his gun
The sound of death echoes
And the rhino drops to the floor

The plains are disrupted
From the shouts of the men
Here to cause disruption
Never to come again

Think he can get away with it
So outrageous rhino's going crazy
He can't run because he is so fat and lazy.

Matthew Skelton (13)
Sheredes Secondary School, Hoddesdon

The Mighty Cheetah

Sprinting silently across the ground searching for his prey,
What's the animal on the menu?
He sets the trap and waits for the moment.
It goes silent for a moment then the silence breaks,
He sprints off as fast as he can be.
The prey desperately scurries away,
It is a desperate struggle as the cheetah wins the kill.
The bone-crunching sound of bone-breaking torture,
The sound of ripping flesh as they tear it to shreds,
So you've heard the mighty creature so please save him.

James Weaver (11)
Sheredes Secondary School, Hoddesdon

Recycle

Recycle, recycle
Paper and shoes
To help save the planet
That we might lose.

We are running out of materials
We cannot make a thing
So we must keep on recycling.

Recycle, recycle
Tins and cans
To help save
Most of the lands.

Don't cut down no more trees
We have enough paper
Don't cut them down
We're asking you please.

Kelly Batchelor (13)
Sheredes Secondary School, Hoddesdon

Rabbit

Jumping like a space hopper,
Down the foggy path,
Out jumps a big brown rabbit,
Says to me, 'Please don't leave me be,
There's a big brown fox, he might eat me raw!
That's him scratching at my door.'
Out jumps a poacher pouncing here and there,
Trying to find a grizzly bear.
But instead he finds a greedy fox,
So he says, 'That's your lot and shoots him on the spot.'

Jazmine Randle (12)
Sheredes Secondary School, Hoddesdon

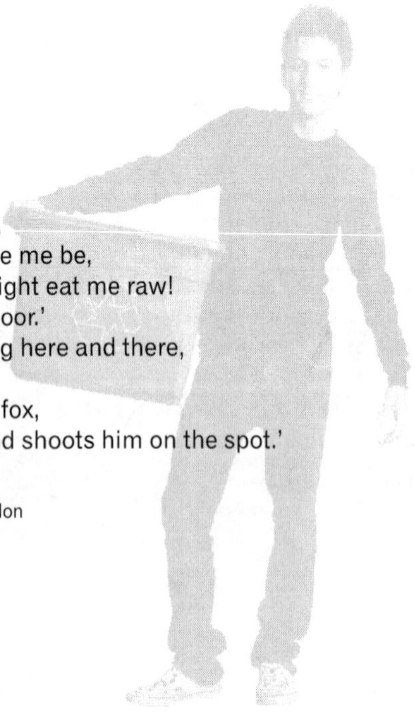

Help The World Today

Pollution is ruining the world today
It is making the sky turn grey
It's turning the planet into a big ashtray
So let's work together and make it go away

If you breathe in it will make you feel ill
Then the doctor will make you take a pill
So do your bit and help today
And make the world be all okay.

Jake Peacock (12)
Sheredes Secondary School, Hoddesdon

Litterbugs!

Litter, litter everywhere
Animals caught in spare
Animals taken from their home
Destroying our ozone.

Without your help it will stay this way
Recycle more and more each day
All over on the floor
Every day there is more and more.

Summer Louise Muir (11)
Sheredes Secondary School, Hoddesdon

Global Warming

Global warming, global warming,
Parts of the world will flood
Taking away the people's precious spuds.
People's homes will get washed away,
There are people sadly saying, 'I've got nowhere to stay!'
Unfortunately people can die; some people are giving a sigh.
So help stop global warming today
And everyone will be happy shouting *hooray!*

Danielle Holt (11)
Sheredes Secondary School, Hoddesdon

Litter, Litter

I hate litter
Don't put it on the floor
'Cause it's killing all the poor
So put it in the bin or you will suffer.

Litter, litter everywhere
Destroying all our ozone layer
Don't kill the animals for heavens sake
Or you will suffer all the hate.

Charlie Rolfe (11)
Sheredes Secondary School, Hoddesdon

Trees And Rubbish - Haikus

Trees
Trees invite the bees
The trees go down, the bees go,
Stop chopping them down.

Rubbish
People drop rubbish,
This affects communities,
Don't do this, bin it!

Charlie Middleton (12)
Sheredes Secondary School, Hoddesdon

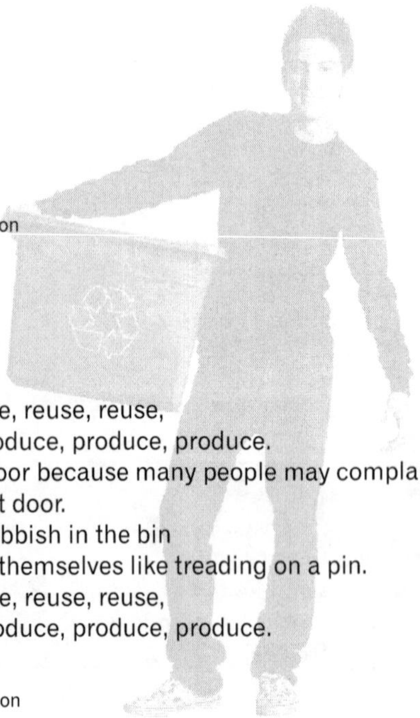

Recycling

Recycle, recycle, recycle, reuse, reuse, reuse,
Do whatever you can do to produce, produce, produce.
Never chuck rubbish on the floor because many people may complain
By knocking right at your front door.
You should always put your rubbish in the bin
Because someone could hurt themselves like treading on a pin.
Recycle, recycle, recycle, reuse, reuse, reuse,
Do whatever you can do to produce, produce, produce.

Kirsty Taylor (11)
Sheredes Secondary School, Hoddesdon

Polar Bear

Swimming through the sea
Searching hard for food
The big polar bear was desperate
It didn't have a clue.
Where have all the fish gone
They have disappeared
Speeding men in fishing boats
Looking very angry.

Tyler Sambrook (12)
Sheredes Secondary School, Hoddesdon

The Environment

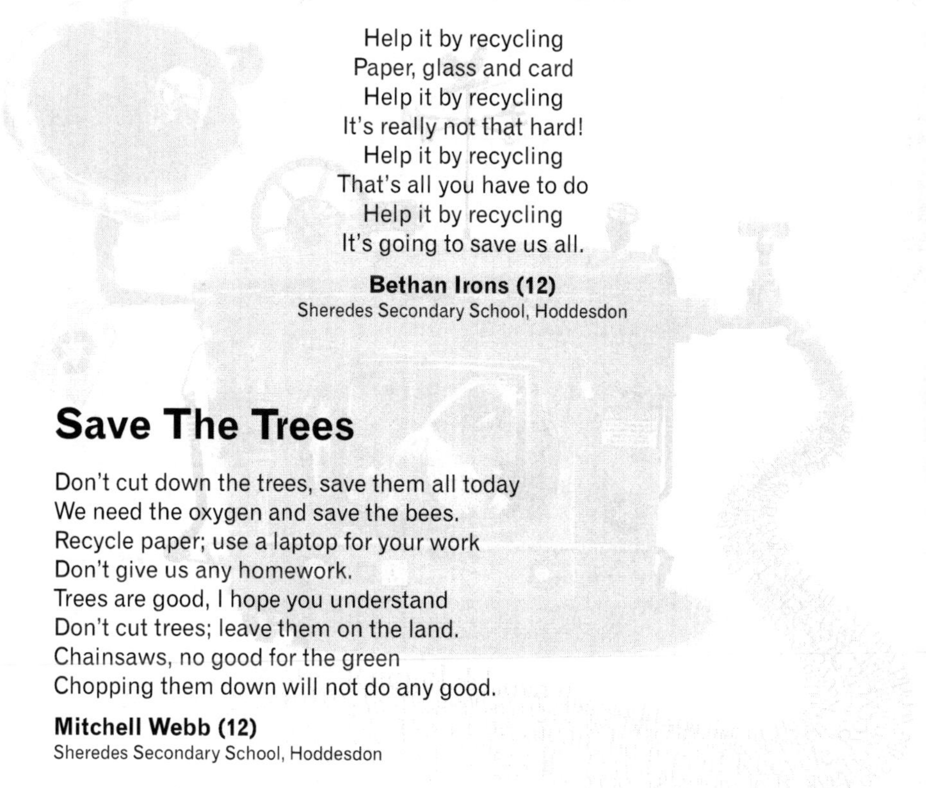

Help it by recycling
Paper, glass and card
Help it by recycling
It's really not that hard!
Help it by recycling
That's all you have to do
Help it by recycling
It's going to save us all.

Bethan Irons (12)
Sheredes Secondary School, Hoddesdon

Save The Trees

Don't cut down the trees, save them all today
We need the oxygen and save the bees.
Recycle paper; use a laptop for your work
Don't give us any homework.
Trees are good, I hope you understand
Don't cut trees; leave them on the land.
Chainsaws, no good for the green
Chopping them down will not do any good.

Mitchell Webb (12)
Sheredes Secondary School, Hoddesdon

Rainforest In The World

All the trees in the world
Being cut down at the speed of light
All the trees in the world
It's giving us all quite a fright.
All the animals in the world
Wondering every day
If they're gonna lose it
All, all, all!

Charlie Egan (11)
Sheredes Secondary School, Hoddesdon

Litter, Litter Everywhere

Litter, litter everywhere,
Animals trapped in despair.
Litter, litter everywhere,
The world looks messy, it needs repair.
Litter, litter everywhere,
If you don't recycle we'll run out of room to put things anywhere.
Litter, litter everywhere,
You'll stop now if you really care.

Melodie Reid (11)
Sheredes Secondary School, Hoddesdon

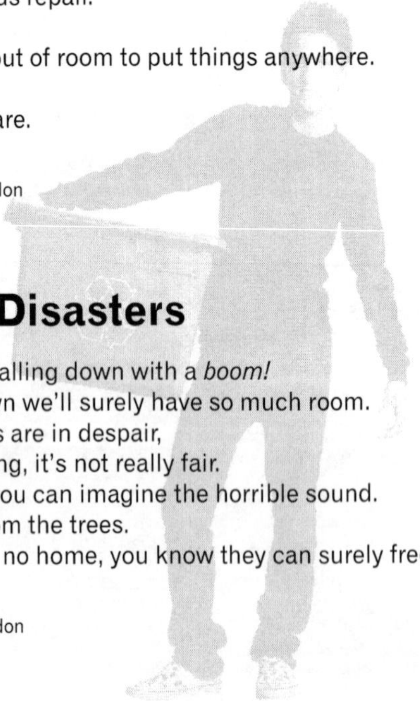

The Rainforest Disasters

All the trees in the world are falling down with a *boom!*
With all the trees coming down we'll surely have so much room.
All the animals in their homes are in despair,
It really is scary and frightening, it's not really fair.
Trees, trees being cut down, you can imagine the horrible sound.
All the oxygen you can get from the trees.
Because all the animals have no home, you know they can surely freeze.

Bailey Stocksley (12)
Sheredes Secondary School, Hoddesdon

Rabbit Hunt

I am a rabbit
People killing for my coat
Here comes a big gun
I think I'd better run
My family's gone
My habitat is ruined
Just for my coat!

Ellie Freeman (11)
Sheredes Secondary School, Hoddesdon

Recycling

Ellie never recycled but she wanted to save the world.
She asked her nan for help; her nan said do this:
'Put away your empty bottles, recycle your paper,

Today's the day to change the world, not for worse, for better!'
Help your country survive and recycle your Five Alive,
Every little counts but helps in big amounts.

Sarah Mockford (12)
Sheredes Secondary School, Hoddesdon

Pollution

Pollution, pollution everywhere
People turning in despair.
Fog is forming into towns
Ready for the acid rain.
Pollution, pollution everywhere
People frozen staring into space.

Bradley Greaves (11)
Sheredes Secondary School, Hoddesdon

Litter Is Bitter

Litter, it is so bad, it is sad.
You can prevent it, just say litter is too bitter
Then *kaboom!* There is so much room
Then you'll be happy so tell your pappy.

Aidan Rosario Piekuta (11)
Sheredes Secondary School, Hoddesdon

Rainforests

Trees are disappearing
They are being cut down
Sent off to factories
In the middle of the town.

Courtney Topley (11)
Sheredes Secondary School, Hoddesdon

Recycling Now! - Haiku

Start recycling now
You're chopping all our trees down
Won't be any left!

Rebecca Suzan (12)
Sheredes Secondary School, Hoddesdon

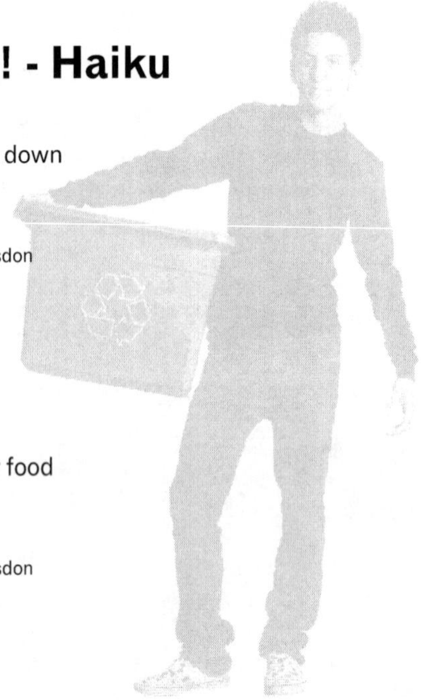

Melt - Haiku

The ice has melted
We kill their homes and their food
They will need our help.

Kelly Pryor (13)
Sheredes Secondary School, Hoddesdon

Polar Bears - Haiku

Polar bears dying
Help us, there's nowhere to live
No food all around.

Jessica Bruton (11)
Sheredes Secondary School, Hoddesdon

Trees - Haiku

People cut trees down
So they will fall to the ground
Just lying around.

Ian Latchford (12)
Sheredes Secondary School, Hoddesdon

Ozone In The Sky

Ozone in the sky
Save us now or we may die
So stop pollution.

Sonny Wise (12)
Sheredes Secondary School, Hoddesdon

In The Windy Breeze

Trees are big and green
Waving in the windy breeze
Stop pollution now!

Tom Dean (12)
Sheredes Secondary School, Hoddesdon

Help Us! - Haiku

Glaciers melting,
Stop! Think, does anyone care?
Help! Don't just sit there.

Libby Barrow (12)
Sheredes Secondary School, Hoddesdon

Rain - Haiku

Acid rain falling
Falling from the cloudy sky
Splashing passers-by.

Matt O'Kelly (12)
Sheredes Secondary School, Hoddesdon

The Layer Of Life - Haiku

We kill the layer
That protects us from the sun
Then we will be none.

Jordan Hodgson (12)
Sheredes Secondary School, Hoddesdon

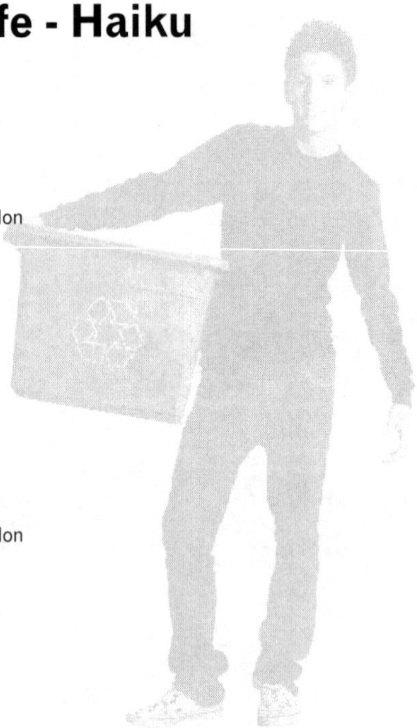

Fire - Haiku

Fire burning wood
It is the end of mankind
The Earth is real still.

Daniel James Knight (12)
Sheredes Secondary School, Hoddesdon

Smoke - Haiku

A puff of black smoke
It glides high up past the sky
Pollution its aim.

Mason Bonura (12)
Sheredes Secondary School, Hoddesdon

Pollution- Haiku

Gases in the air
There are gases everywhere
Pollution will kill.

Rebecca Clohosy (12)
Sheredes Secondary School, Hoddesdon

Hurricanes - Haiku

Hurricane and winds
Spreading through the continents
Taking every life.

Mollie Cole (13)
Sheredes Secondary School, Hoddesdon

The Big Melt - Haiku

Ice caps are melting
Sea levels are rising up
What will happen next?

Harry Allen
Sheredes Secondary School, Hoddesdon

Tsunami Haiku

A monstrous wave
Drowning everything in sight
Taking every life.

Bronwyn Scholes (12)
Sheredes Secondary School, Hoddesdon

Environmental - Haiku

You must recycle
Because you are killing the
Ozone please save me.

Rhys Andrew Sayers-Jones (12)
Sheredes Secondary School, Hoddesdon

Forest Fire - Haiku

The woods are now dead
Everything is black and shed
The mammals have fled.

Nick Horton (13)
Sheredes Secondary School, Hoddesdon

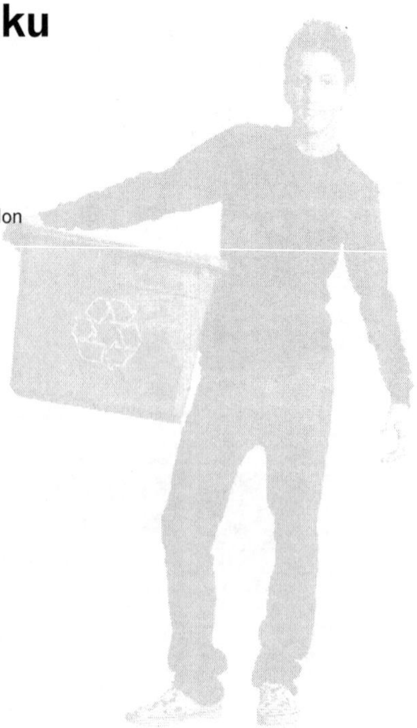

Why?

We stereotype and predict,
We assume and accuse.
Why?
We fear but do not understand,
We see others as we want to see them.
Why?
You see a person on the street,
You instantly see their colour.
Why?
We have energy saving ideas
But keep the budget needed for them.
Why?
I do not fear the dark but keep the lights on anyway.
The novelty of my pet has worn off so I give it away.
Why?
We laugh and we cry, we learn
Where we went wrong and correct mistakes.
Why?
We band together and help one another,
Individuality no longer matters, we finally care.
Why?
Because we are human!

Connor Sims (15)
Stalham High School, Stalham

Pass The Blame

Toxic gas fills our skies,
Hungry children start to cry,
Everyone wants to help but no one says
It was me.
They pass the blame.

Dogs hungry from lack of food,
But the owner is not in the mood,
No one helps.
It wasn't me.
They pass the blame.

Rainforests dying, no trees left.
Soldiers dying, no heroes left.
No one goes to help,
It wasn't me.
They pass the blame.

If only they said it was me!
It would be better.

Bethany Sarah Younge (14)
Stalham High School, Stalham

Broken

Frozen. Bitter. Broken.
Ice-aged bones stiffened on nights like this.
A runaway is never welcomed.
A runaway is never beckoned.
Fragile. Broke. Beaten.
Haunted dreams plagued Christmas midnights.
Never had a choice but to flee.
Never chose to live a life destitute of glee.
Not Third World, not a greenhouse gas, not a prisoner,
Not important to governments, to society, to families.

Sarah Bean (17)
Stratton Upper School, Biggleswade

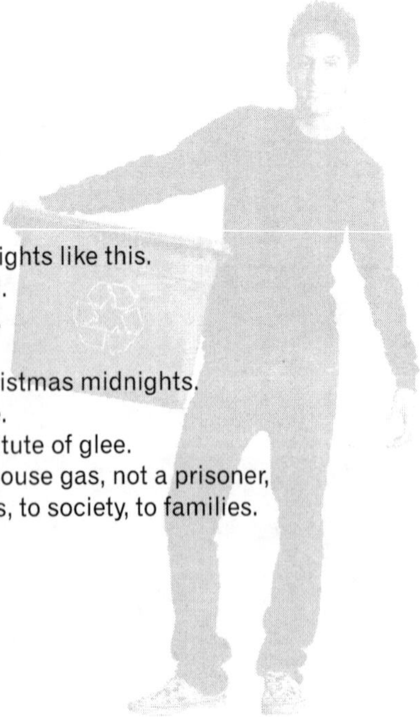

There Was Once A Planet Called Earth

There was once a planet called Earth
That was a peaceful place at first
Then Man came along
And the Earth got seriously hurt.

The sea levels rose
As the Gulf Stream began to close
And the wind blew to and fro
Then it began to snow.

It grew colder and colder
The snow was up to my shoulder
The birds began to drown
And we didn't know what to do!

Then one morning
When the sun was just dawning
Earth's population none
Because we were all gone!
Isn't that nice?

Dana McConkey (13)
Stratton Upper School, Biggleswade

Pollution

We give you fresh air
You give us dirt and grime
In the air from planes and cars
We all choke on your dirt and grime.

Antony Carter (13)
Stratton Upper School, Biggleswade

Our Dying Earth

Resources are depleted
Rainforests deleted
The forecast of the world is foretold
The future is set to be cold
Earth has its right
But we can't see that in our sights.

Animals are leaving fast
We are naïve to think they will last
Wind, water, fire, earth, air
Soon there will be none anywhere
Habitats have no choice
They must move as they have no voice.

The Earth frowns
As it looks down
At its creations lying on the ground.
Earth is the only home we know
If we destroy it, there is no place to go
Will we ever see the day it will once again grow?

The world is becoming less dense
To fix it money is at an expense
Because people are breaking its defence
Just like wind does to a garden fence.
If we all pitch in
Such as recycling instead of putting everything in the bin
Maybe the world will become a better place
I wish this problem were not so hard to face.

I am not here to deceive
United we can achieve
So future generations will not have to grieve!

Tanvir Kabir (13)
The Chadwell Heath Foundation School, Romford

Why?

My question is . . .
Why abuse?
Why mistreat?
Why leave your refuse on the street?
Your selfish actions overheat
Why trample beauty beneath your feet?

Why make this world an ugly place?
Why cut down the rainforest on my face?
Why merrily kill me in your haste
To live your life at an easy pace
Destroying the home of the human race?

Why cut the throat of your fellow man?
Why invade, just because you can?
Why ruin the world with your evil plan
Murdering people as they ran?

Why let earthlings fade away?
Why let starvation happen today?
Don't let wealth lead the way
And let the starving have their say.

My beauty is amazing
My ground was once outstanding
Before you people started landing
Now you have ruined my surroundings.

Sarah Leanne Smith (13)
The Chadwell Heath Foundation School, Romford

Alone

Living on the street, don't know where to go,
Nobody cares, nobody knows.
People look at me from above,
But all I really want is love.

Nobody understands.
They think I'm just a has been from a band.
Looking at me like, oh what a fool!
But all I want to show them is that I can still be cool.

I see people that I used to call friends around,
They act like they don't know.
Is there anyone that can lend a hand
So I can give life a go?

As I lie here on the floor
Looking up into the stars,
Thinking what it would be like to have a home with clothes,
Where did I go wrong?

Lauren Sophia Goddard (14)
The Chadwell Heath Foundation School, Romford

The Ticking Clock

Earth: Time is running out my friends
Humans: You fool; we're nowhere near the end.
Earth: But if you continue with your ways
Humans: What! It'll be the last of our days?
Earth: You cut down trees without a care and watch as oceans weep in despair.
Humans: But do you really think there is a human that does truly care?
Earth: You still have time to realise the damage you've done and compromise.
Humans: There is no space for compromise
There is no time to stop and stare at what you think we should show care!
Earth: The environment is on its knees, the atmosphere is to its teeth,
Please listen to my crying please and make this selfish madness cease!

Jamell Ivan Samuels (13)
The Chadwell Heath Foundation School, Romford

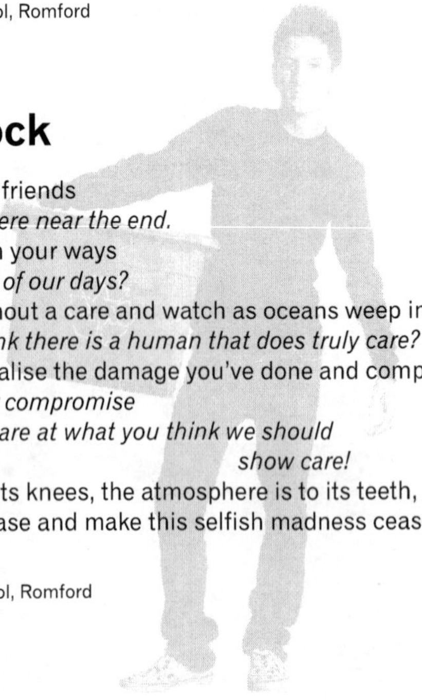

The Canal

I see a polluted canal
And think how did it get so bad
All of the rubbish piled on top of each other
How did it get so foul?

I walk past and I see
The trees surrounding me
Litter on the ground everywhere
This sight I can no longer bear.

All the things God gave us
Wonderful gifts
And we turn them into dust
We should not do this.

I see a polluted canal
It's screaming out loud to me
Like a crying baby
Help me, help me please!

Lauren Peta Cook (13)
The Chadwell Heath Foundation School, Romford

In My Car

In my car, not going far
There's a sight, a person on his bike
He must be having fun in the sun
There I see him going so far
Whereas I'm still in my car
He's in the open air which I cannot bear
Sitting in my car not going that far
Living this way is the price to pay
With so many things to do, my life is just like a zoo
His trip is getting shorter
While mine is getting longer
His ride is free while I'm trying to pay my driving fee
He smells the fresh air
While I smell the poisonous air
I'm in my car not going far.

Haroon Ikram (13)
The Chadwell Heath Foundation School, Romford

The Mess Of The World

The poverty in the world is not a pretty sight,
It makes me fight for their rights.
The helpless children of the universe
Will try to defeat that dirty curse.

We are causing the pollution,
But no one knows the solution.
Cars are just a happy joy,
They are the terrible ploy.

Animals are getting extinct,
But they do not know that we are the jinx.
The lions used to be roaring,
But now they know their future is boring, snoring.

Deforestation is ruining the tribes
So they have no culture to describe.
The trees are worth more than the money,
But everyone thinks that is so funny.

Gokulann Anantharnajan (13)
The Chadwell Heath Foundation School, Romford

The Price Of War

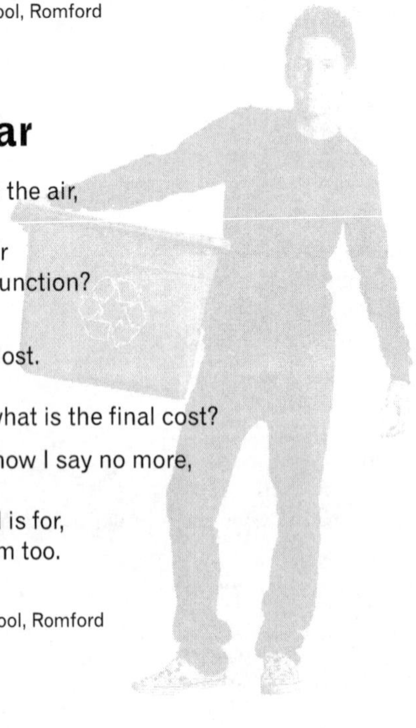

A single bullet flying through the air,
Flying to destruction.
Is this really what you call fair
In a world too aggressive to function?

All around a world of war,
A punch, a kick, another life lost.
But yet I ask, what is it for?
All this still happening, but what is the final cost?

I have talked and talked but now I say no more,
The rest is up to you.
Consider everyone this world is for,
Not just you, but me and them too.

Jasveen Bansal (13)
The Chadwell Heath Foundation School, Romford

The Trees Last Day

There is just another tree
Sitting there thinking it's free.
In its own world lost in the wild
Feeling the wind, not hot nor mild.

When the cranes come to cut it down
All the tree can do is give a frown.
It gets cut down without a choice
It would scream if it had a voice.

The top is taken and the bottom is left
Cutting it down is a life theft.
To make paper, taking a life is cold
A tree dies every time you see paper unfold.

If you met a tree it would say
I'm living my last night today.
Tomorrow I'll die so it's time for goodbyes
Because tomorrow I won't see the sunrise.

Ali Choudhury (13)
The Chadwell Heath Foundation School, Romford

The Weeping Earth

You treat me like a rubbish bin
Why make this world such a sin?
Sooner or later the world will end
But it's never too late to make amends.
You cut down trees without a care
And watch as oceans weep in despair.
You stand around and watch me dying
Instead of saving my life, you watch me crying.
You pollute the air leaving me out of breath
Not realising you're choking me to death.
So make amends and be clever
So I can live forever and ever.

Tara-Louise Williams (13)
The Chadwell Heath Foundation School, Romford

A Bliss Waters End

The water's always on, makes me think what's going on.
I say to the people *someone could use that*
Then follow it up with *don't abuse that.*
Killing the planet is what you are doing,
Turning it into such a ruin.
Take the people in those poor countries, no water, no bread,
No treats before bed.
No pennies for a poppy, no pennies for bread,
Think of the charities that said we need cred.
So much greed, so much hate,
Unlike our school fete.
Pick up that litter; wipe up your spit,
Some of this stuff is not legit.
Killing the planet, killing the trees,
There goes the rainforests and all the bees.
Landfills going up, landfills going down,
You're killing the planet, open your eyes!

Colynn Adamson (14)
The Chadwell Heath Foundation School, Romford

Untitled

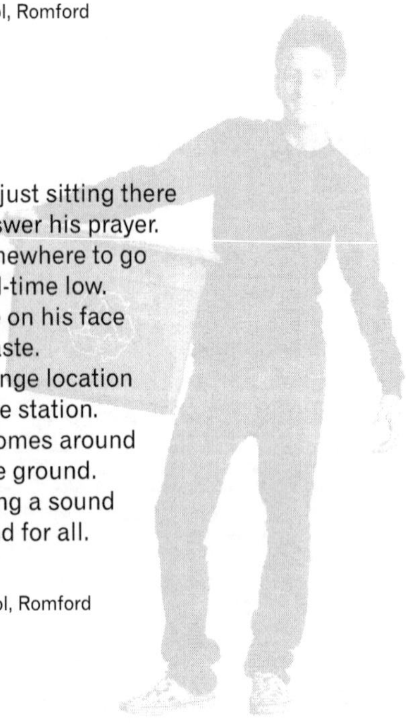

Walking along the street, he's just sitting there
Just a bit of change would answer his prayer.
Everyone around him, has somewhere to go
But not this man, he's at an all-time low.
Even just a penny puts a smile on his face
His life is in danger, what a waste.
Not the energy to move or change location
There he is again, sitting by the station.
He starts to shiver as winter comes around
Next day I see him lying on the ground.
Motionless as sleep, not making a sound
He came to his death, once and for all.

Mitchell Omer (14)
The Chadwell Heath Foundation School, Romford

Waste

What a waste this war has brought on us,
What a waste of life this war has brought on us,
What a waste of time this war has brought on us,
What a waste of money this war has brought on us.

What a waste of money this war has brought on us,
This money they use to fight and kill people
Could be used to help and revive people,
The money they pay to steal people's land
Could have been the money put in an African's hand.

What a waste this war has brought on us,
What a waste of life this war has brought on us,
What a waste of time this war has brought on us,
What a waste of money this war has brought on us.

What a waste of time this war has brought on us,
All this time they wasted killing and destroying people's lives
Should have been used to help the poor.
It would be nice for all those men to go and see their wives.

What a waste this war has brought on us,
What a waste of life this war has brought on us,
What a waste of time this war has brought on us,
What a waste of money this war has brought on us.

What a waste of life this war has brought on us,
Life is such a beautiful thing that it causes such pain when it is taken away.
You get a horrible pain in your heart
And for the rest of your life you feel there's something to say.

What a waste this war has brought on us,
What a waste of life this war has brought on us,
What a waste of time this war has brought on us,
What a waste of money this war has brought on us.

Molly Freeman (11)
The Nobel School, Stevenage

War, War, War

War, war, war,
It's not a laughing matter.

Families, families, families,
Getting even sadder.

Civilians, civilians, civilians,
What have they done wrong?

Years, years, years,
It's becoming way too long.

A game, a game, a game,
It goes from advantage back to deuce.

Peace, peace, peace,
Why can't we just call a truce?

Death, death, death,
Thousands of soldiers are dying.

Pain, pain, pain,
All the suffering and crying.

Bang, bang, bang
Another soldier's dead.

It's true, it's true, it's true
The news his comrades dread.

When, when, when
Will this war end?

Fight, fight, fight,
How long will our boys defend

War, war, war,
It's not a laughing matter!

Sam Lucey (11)
The Nobel School, Stevenage

War Is War

Bang! Bang!
All that we hear,
Killing people,
No sound of a cheer,
Watching the gravestones piling up.
Killing sprees,
Bloodstained knives,
Losing people.
Dead!

I'm riding my bicycle down the long street
Then suddenly a bomb blows up at my feet.
I'm feeling scared,
Don't know what to do
Until I realise
It only took off my shoe.

There are no houses to shelter in,
All that's around me is a smelly bin.
There's no one around to calm down your pain,
Most of these are dead, such a shame.

War isn't good,
Not good at all.
So if you want to feel like I am today,
Try to stop war
And you'll be OK.

James White (11)
The Nobel School, Stevenage

Animals

A nimals need a good environment to live
N ever abuse animals
I nnocent animals
M ake-up should not be tested on them
A nimals should be set free
L et the animals live in peace
S ave the animals.

Grace Carter (11)
The Nobel School, Stevenage

World Poem

Melting ice caps everywhere.
Endangered species, pandas, tigers, polar bears
Litter all over the ground
Piled in an untidy mound.
It's a lovely world to live,
So why do people damage it?

Pollution fumes fly around,
Children falling to the ground,
Disease spreading everywhere
People cough and splutter in despair.
It's a lovely world to live
So why do people damage it?

Homes are getting destroyed,
People are getting annoyed,
They have nowhere to go,
Nowhere to shelter from rain, sleet and snow.
It's a lovely world to live
So why do people damage it?

But there's something we can do,
Walk everywhere we can, use a bin too,
Together we can help the world.
It's a lovely world to live
And now we can save it!

Rebecca Fry (11)
The Nobel School, Stevenage

Recycle

R ecycle as much as you can
E verybody can recycle so do it!
C ardboard can be recycled, so can plastic such as yoghurt pots, milk cartons and many more
Y ou can do it, recycle!
C lothes, shoes and paper can be recycled
L earn more about recycling and do all you can
E verybody can recycle so everybody *should* recycle.

Katie Sollis (11)
The Nobel School, Stevenage

Terrorism

Ignorance x fear
= Terror

Terror x pressure
= Mistakes

Mistakes x people
= Devastation.

Devastation x exposure
= Death

Death x knowledge
= Weapons

Weapons x power
= Destruction

Destruction x revenge
= War

War x Man
= Resistance

Resistance x technology
= Terrorism

Terrorism x faith
= Ignorance.

Michael Francis (13)
The Nobel School, Stevenage

Recycle

R ecycle anything you can
E verything that can be recycled recycle it
C ardboard, clothes, shoes as well
Y oghurt pots, milk bottles and even old TVs
C ans, glass and paper too
L earn about recycling and don't use our planet as a rubbish bin!
E verything that can be recycled recycle it

Anyone can recycle, even you, recycle!

Jessica Dutt (11)
The Nobel School, Stevenage

Why Should There Be Poverty And War?

Hollow faces of famine and fear
Children starving and dying each day
Parents cry for help
As they watch their child/children die

Soldiers march into war shattered towns
Killing innocent people like animals
Burning down their only hope
With fragile houses littering the street
And wounded bodies lie scattered around.

Oh people of my nation
Please give to the needy; we must stop the war in our world
We've got to say goodbye to poverty
Goodbye poverty
We say goodbye to you.

Poverty we no longer need you
We have had enough of a hard time
Your purpose was to make sure that we wouldn't make it so far.

Oh people of my nation
Please give to the needy; we must stop the war in our world
We've got to say goodbye to poverty
Goodbye poverty
We say goodbye to you.

Abigail Ativie (11)
The Nobel School, Stevenage

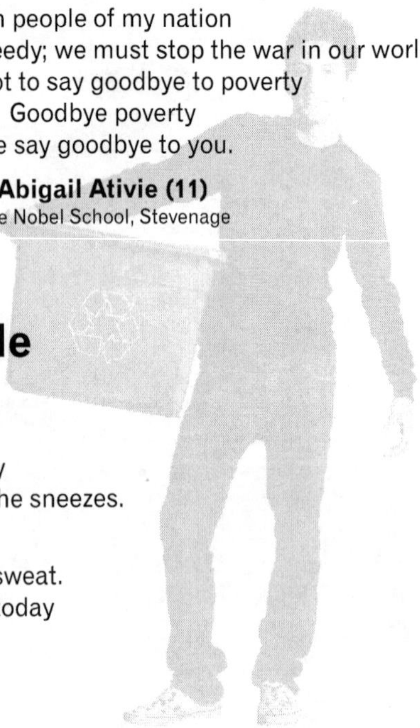

Homeless People

All these people on the street
Wearing nothing on their feet
Drinking water, dark and misty
Having diseases and getting the sneezes.

Streets are cold and wet
And they can't clean up their sweat.
So help the homeless people today
And it will make their day.

Danielle Murphy (11)
The Nobel School, Stevenage

Stop Global Warming

Ice caps are melting
Polar bears dying
Pollution in the streets
Causing too much heat.

Stop global warming
Before we're all extinct!

Global wars beginning
Causing killings to harmless humans
Forest being erased
No oxygen for us to breathe.

Stop global warming
Before we're all extinct!

Animals close to extinction
Just for their skin
Energy being used
Causing CO_2
Causing climate change.

Stop global warming
Before we're all extinct!
It's in *your* hands!

Alex Topham (12)
The Nobel School, Stevenage

No One Likes War - Haiku

War, war is not good
A war kills lots of people
Really, please stop wars.

Tom Harris (11)
The Nobel School, Stevenage

Our World

Think of a world without any trees
Flowers and birds, sunset and seas.
These things around us we have enjoyed
But because of our selfishness are being destroyed.
We fill up the skies with toxins and smoke
And don't seem to care that our planet will choke.
Without even thinking we throw things away
Causing landfills to grow with rot and decay.
We're chopping down trees for furniture production
Causing pandas and other animals all sorts of disruption.
We take things from countries who have nothing to give
To satisfy our greed while they struggle to live.
It is time for us all to find a solution
Instead of continually filling this world with pollution.
We need to think about our actions each day
And try and recycle instead of throwing away.
Instead of us always driving the car
We could bike or walk if it isn't too far.
Using less water and turning off the light
Is just the beginning of the climate change fight.
Looking after our planet is important to do
Because God created this world for me and for you.

Annabelle Shortland (11)
The Nobel School, Stevenage

Too Much For The World

The world is a delicate place,
It needs to be looked after with special care
Because if we don't take action soon,
The world will soon not be there.

Mid autumn breeze blowing heavily
As you take a stroll down the street.
Into the park you turn,
To find litter blowing round your feet.

Cars are racing past you,
And it's a boiling hot day.
Why can't they be walking
Instead of blowing their steam away?

The climate is changing quicker,
Quicker than you think
And soon in the blink of an eye
The world will be extinct.

What's so hard about recycling?
It's putting our rubbish to good use,
So please remember these three words.
Reuse, recycle, reduce.

Paige Stevens (11)
The Nobel School, Stevenage

Animals And Extinction

With animals' lives to spare
You share the poor animals' hair
Their thoughts and feelings
You will never know.

You would never treat a person like that
So why are you treating animals like that?
Think about it
You will never know.

You wouldn't like to be in a cage
So why are you putting them in a cage?
For what will you achieve
You will never know.

Animals don't live long
So why are you making their poor lives short?
The misery they go through
You will never know.

All time and pain
No fun and games
How has it come to this?
Well, I guess *you* should find some answers then.

Chloe Robbins (12)
The Nobel School, Stevenage

What Is Wrong With The World?

Everything has gone wrong,
The ice caps are melting soon they'll be gone!
All my favourite animals, furry, slimy or fast,
Are leaving the planet, soon my cat will be last!

Racism hit me like a pole,
Someone called my friend, 'black as coal'
I couldn't breathe when I went to school,
Mum said, 'It's pollution from car fuel.'

I watched television the other night,
And found people crying in fright.
Their homes had been destroyed by a natural disaster,
They keep on happening and people are dying faster.

I've seen homeless people sleeping on the streets,
With nothing to keep them warm except thin sheets.
They haven't got a nice warm home like us,
Sometimes they have to sleep on the bus!

Now I've told you things we need to change,
We should get a move on before the planet gets rearranged!
So please help us to help the planet now,
When you have you'll realise what you did and say *wow!*

Lily Edwards (11)
The Nobel School, Stevenage

Pollution, Pollution

Pollution, pollution,
Oh horrible pollution,
The thing that we all hate.
It's destroying the trees and environment,
It's definitely not our mate!

Pollution, pollution,
Oh horrible pollution.
Soon the ozone layer will be gone
And the world will become so polluted,
The Earth will be none.

Pollution, pollution,
Oh horrible pollution,
The smoke puffing up in the air,
And the sky thickening with smoke.
We need to be aware.

Pollution, pollution,
Oh horrible pollution,
It needs to stop now
To save lives and our planet.
We will do it somehow!

Amy Nugent (11)
The Nobel School, Stevenage

If The World Was Big And Green

If the world was big and green each house would have solar panels
on the roof.
If the world was big and green the rainforests would be huge and living.
If the world was big and green there would be no litter and rubbish
on the ground.
If the world was big and green polar bears would have a safe place to live.
If the world was big and green each street would have a recycling area.
If the world was big and green everyone would be treated in the same way.
If the world was big and green everything would be perfect.

Sophie Taylor (11)
The Nobel School, Stevenage

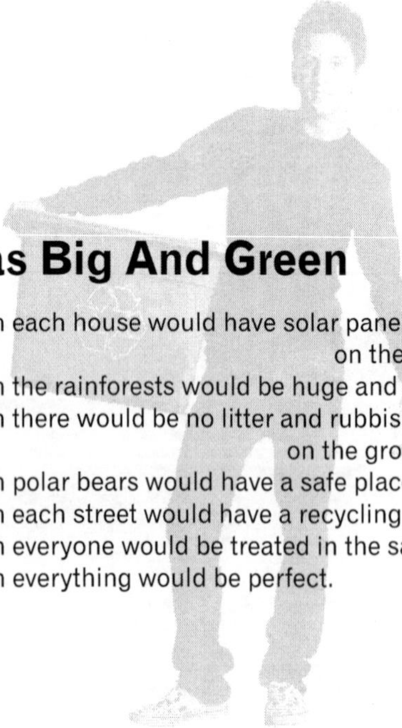

Save Our World

Listen up everyone
Something serious has to be done.
As you go about your busy lives just stop and think
What you can do to bring our world back from the brink.
Too much smoke and smog is sad
But nice clean air won't make you bad.
The seas are rising and the land is in ruins
The ice caps are melting, what are we doing?
All the wars that are going on
Just because people don't get along.
Do you know how mad this makes me feel?
But to some people it's no big deal.
Animals are struggling to survive
It's in our power to help them thrive.
This is our chance to make a difference, so come on, shout out loud
And make yourself feel really proud.
A little thought is all it takes
To help preserve our land, the skies and lakes.
So think about our world out there
I don't believe you do not care
You wouldn't dare!

Katie Elliott (12)
The Nobel School, Stevenage

Environment

Save the environment together, help!
Don't be a lazy bones, get up off your rear
Save the environment don't let it disappear.
You don't have to go mad, just lend a hand
And help save Antarctica and save the snow land
This isn't a quiz but what would you say?
Pollution is a death trap waiting to be laid
Losing species every day
Who would want to stay this way?
So help me save this unique planet
From destruction, devastation and death.

Danielle Callister (11)
The Nobel School, Stevenage

Making A Difference

Pollution is bad, it's destroying the world
Ozone layer's breaking away
The ice caps are melting
The animals are dying
Soon our world will be flooded.

Why is there war? People get hurt
People are dying, bullets are flying
All because they don't get along
What is the point of war?

Pandas, elephants are so great
Why should we see them suffer?
We kill them just for food.
What we gonna do if they go extinct?

We litter the streets as if it's a bin
You see it everywhere, on the road in the park,
Why should other people clean it up
When it's other people's actions?
So use the thing next to you, a bin!

Daniel Hudson (11)
The Nobel School, Stevenage

War

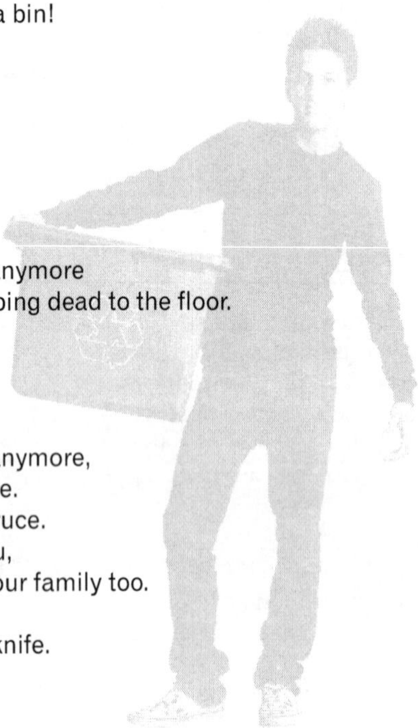

War, war, war, we don't want anymore
People getting shot and dropping dead to the floor.
Air force flying,
Citizens dying,
Families crying,
Soldiers trying,
War, war, war, we don't want anymore,
Can't stand the blood and gore.
Let's let it all lose and call a truce.
Look at the people around you,
You wouldn't like it if it was your family too.
People want to live their life
Not get shot or stabbed by a knife.

George Hepburn (11)
The Nobel School, Stevenage

The War Cycle

Weapons x power
= Ignorance

Ignorance x pride
= Foolishness

Foolishness x strength
= War

War x bombs
= Death

Death x people
= Slaughter

Slaughter x wealth
= Business

Business x corruption
= Greed

Greed x technology
= Weapons.

Harry Mitchell (13)
The Nobel School, Stevenage

Rubbish, Rubbish, Rubbish

Rubbish being thrown on the floor
When there is a rubbish bin right next door.
Crisp packets, cans lying all around,
Being kicked in the air and falling on the ground.

Chewing gum stuck under the seat
Sweet wrappers glued to your feet.
Dead animals stuck in cans
More will die before you can say, 'My name is Sam!'

Sewage blocks in pipes and drains
Just like power cuts shut off the mains.
What can we do to save the world
Or do we have Earth's future sold?

Chloe Legrand (11)
The Nobel School, Stevenage

The Pollution Solution

How do we stop?
It's getting worse day by day
I wish we could use a mop
And clear it all away
The animals are dying
The rainforests are rotting away
People are lying
They're dropping litter every day
We feel the wind rushing on our feet, in the park
And the same thing happens on the street, we hear dogs bark
And we see the bright sun
We know that our job is done
When we can walk along the street
With our feet
We've got to stop
And make it better each day
We'll even use a mop
To clear it all away.

Fiza Raza (11)
The Nobel School, Stevenage

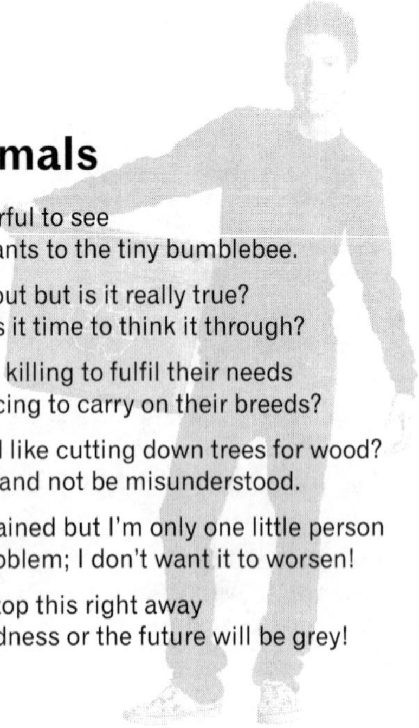

Endangered Animals

Animals, animals, how wonderful to see
From the strong mighty elephants to the tiny bumblebee.

Extinction is always talked about but is it really true?
Are the animals really dying, is it time to think it through?

Is it the poachers that keep on killing to fulfil their needs
Or are the animal not reproducing to carry on their breeds?

Are their habitats being ruined like cutting down trees for wood?
We need to make a difference and not be misunderstood.

It's everything I have just explained but I'm only one little person
Everyone needs to help the problem; I don't want it to worsen!

So all I have to say is please stop this right away
Stop this cruelty, stop this madness or the future will be grey!

Rosie Kay (11)
The Nobel School, Stevenage

Environments Changing

Where are our ice lands?
The air is warming
Big ice caps are melting
The water levels are rising
Polar bears' habitats are being destroyed
Where will they live?

Rainforests disappearing
Trees being cut down
No food to eat
Temperatures are rising
Animals have no place to live
Where is the water
Diseases in the soil
Animals are dying of dehydration
Poachers are killing for meat and fur
Making some animals extinct
People are dying from dirty diseased water.

Oliver Smith (11)
The Nobel School, Stevenage

Hidden Monsters

Monsters are everywhere,
In every dustbin bag,
On every child-made clothes tag,
In the pollution, in the air,
Monsters are everywhere.

In the tanks that go out to war,
In the wood on your door,
In the litter on the ground,
In even the pollution of sound,
Monsters are everywhere.

But to me the resolution is very clear
To have a clean and happy new year.
So the animals don't wail and our purse strings don't tug,
The one thing everybody needs is a great big hug.

Emily Price (11)
The Nobel School, Stevenage

Reduce, Reuse, Recycle

Reduce is the first thing
Don't put it on the floor
Buy objects with less packaging
Please put it in the bin.

Reuse is second
Turn a box into a house
Use the opposite side of the paper
Build a toy for a mouse.

Recycle is last but not least
Cans and paper in the blue bin
Put glass into the red
Otherwise you shall live life in sin.

Those are the key points
For living your life happy
Keep the world nice
And for generations after it'll still be here.

Kayleigh Harris (12)
The Nobel School, Stevenage

Day By Day

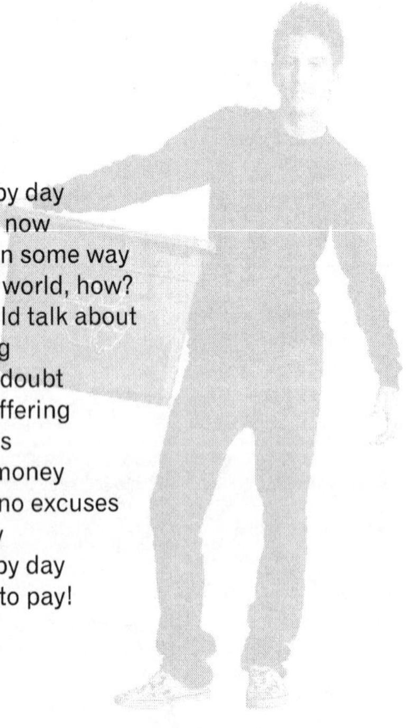

Pollution is getting worse day by day
We need to take serious action now
We need to make a difference in some way
How do you expect to save the world, how?
There are so many things I could talk about
So now I will talk about littering
We drop lots of litter without a doubt
And by the end we could be suffering
Now I will talk about water uses
Showers are better for saving money
I hope you will help the world, no excuses
This is serious and is not funny
Pollution is getting worse day by day
By the end you will be the one to pay!

Nicola Parker (11)
The Nobel School, Stevenage

Animal Cruelty

With broken bones and painful sights
Nets close over me to block my light.
Thrown in a cage they turn the key
Oh how could this be done to me?

I look upon my life and world
I lay in my basket tightly curled.
I never get cleaned, I have fleas
Oh how could this be done to me?

Why would they, I've done nothing wrong
Apart from the occasional pong.
Looking after me there's no fee
Oh how could this be done to me?

I can't go on, I need some help
Until I'm hurt again, then I yelp.
How understated they must be
Oh how could this be done to me.

Amy Jackson (12)
The Nobel School, Stevenage

We Can Make Changes!

You're lucky not panicking every day
With young children working, no school, no fun.
Not able to share their most crucial say.
People suffering from the boiling sun,
Planes flying, souls dying, bombs falling, why?
Grieving families have lost a loved one.
All this starts with greed, making people cry.
They dream of it ending, where we have won.
No fresh air anymore, no clear blue sky.
Where are those beautiful winters so white?
We're just too lazy to give it a try.
Just thinking of world's end gives me a fright.
What's happening? We can make a difference
If only as people we could see sense!

Leanna Campbell (11)
The Nobel School, Stevenage

Destroying Life

Rainforests being cut down by the minute
A person being slain by a small piercing knife
Beautiful animals close to extinction
Yes, we're destroying life!

The sun has set an hour early
The smoke is rising from a newly lit bonfire
Animals fleeing their burning homes
Yes, we're destroying our heart's desire.

Landscapes being ruined with litter
There's nothing else to see
There's no kindness left in this land
Yes, what are we?

No civilized things left to say
Sitting back and being lazy
Letting other people destroy this land
Yes, how lazy are we!

Rachel Garner (11)
The Nobel School, Stevenage

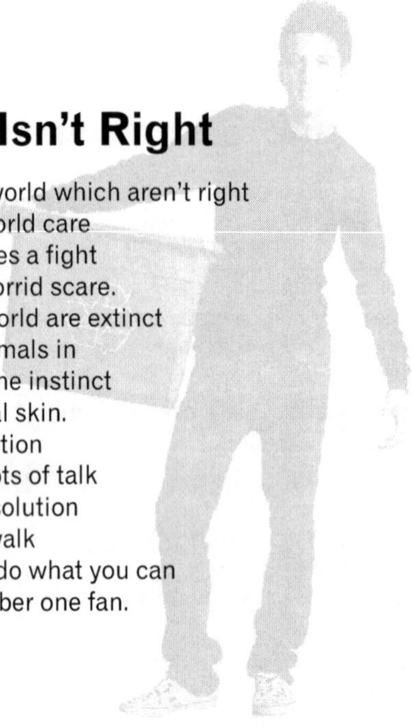

Why The World Isn't Right

There are some things in the world which aren't right
And not many people in the world care
People try and help but it makes a fight
And what could happen is a horrid scare.
Like so many animals in the world are extinct
So let's try and keep some animals in
Everyone should have or feel the instinct
So don't go out and buy animal skin.
One other problem is the pollution
There is not much worry but lots of talk
So let's come up with a good solution
So please could you cycle or walk
So please could you help and do what you can
And then I would be your number one fan.

Emma Rodgers (11)
The Nobel School, Stevenage

Save The Planet

Our world is precious but we abuse it
Resources are going but we still use it.

In a perfect world we would all recycle
Not the car – use a bicycle.

Fight wars on litter not on people
Look after nature – save the beetle.

Fossil fuels are running out
But still not many of us shout.

Turn down the heating, wear an extra layer
Every time makes you less of a slayer.

Unplug, turn off, don't leave on standby
Or one day you will say goodbye.

Save the planet, don't be sad
Hope one day you'll make us glad.

Jessica-Mai Seales (12)
The Nobel School, Stevenage

If I'm Homeless You're Rich

If I smell pollution you smell fragrance
If I sit on the ground you, sit on chairs
If I hear traffic you hear the great prance
If I eat nothing you eat fresh pears.

If I taste bitterness you taste rich meat
If I try to earn you have cash in pockets
If I touch ice you touch the playful sleet
If I look at cars you check your rockets.

If I see I'm homeless you see you're rich
If I feel tension you feel calm and peace
If I say nothing you be a big snitch
If I don't spray my hair you put on grease.

These poor homeless people have nothing - think!
Now it is time for us to do something.

Nabiha Chowdhury (11)
The Nobel School, Stevenage

Save The Polar Bears

Another polar bear dies
Another iceberg melts away
But no one answers our cries
We Arctic creatures don't get our say.

We're losing our entire world
But no one really cares
No one will try to help the last of the polar bears.

We are real creatures
With fur, with teeth and claws
But what we really need to know is
Who will fight for our cause?

Who will save the polar bears?
Don't let us go extinct
All we ask is that you
Just stop, sit down and think!

Summer Eid (11)
The Nobel School, Stevenage

Superman Can't Save Us

This is insane
Soldiers are dying
People in pain
Family all crying
But Superman can't save us!

Stop trees being cut down
Stop the animals dying
Recycle paper in your town
Smoke flying
But Superman can't save us!

United we stand
To end this war
Altogether hand in hand
To help the poor
Then Superman won't need to save us!

Amy Clynes (11)
The Nobel School, Stevenage

Save Our World!

Have you ever got hurt? Now the world is too
Pollution can kill, especially our Earth.
Why would you want a soft leopard skin shoe?
Polluting will change the grass into mould.

You want to make a change? Then recycle!
Don't be a litterbug, it's very bad
Do not use a car, ride a bicycle
Litter is turning the world really mad!

War is horrible; it's a waste of time
Calling people names is not very nice.
Fighting kills thousands and it is a crime
You will make them feel as freezing as ice.

Come on kids, it's our time to smile and shine
Why live our cool lives like this all the time?

Holly Ingram (11)
The Nobel School, Stevenage

The Death Of The Polar Bear

The polar caps are melting
The polar bear will die
The atmosphere is heating up
The Arctic is soon to fry.

Bears can't swim forever
They all will surely sink
Can't we stop this madness?
Can't we stop and think?

The fate of a species
Rests in our hands
The end of the polar bear
And their Arctic lands.

Andrew Stephens (11)
The Nobel School, Stevenage

Just Think About It

The world's a state
Rainforests cut down at a quick rate.
Poverty and famine is here, it's time to act
Being homeless is more common and that's a fact.
Pollution's in the air
Wars going on everywhere.
Recycling is up and litter's down
The perfect words for a town.
Racism makes people sad
Extinction and death of animals is totally mad.
We must change and make a difference fast
In this state the world will never last.

Jack Manning (12)
The Nobel School, Stevenage

The World

I'm trying to write a poem for the big green machine
But I can't think of one single thing!
There is always more pollution in the air
But everyone acts like they don't even care.

People with guns and knives are really bad,
They murder us and make me feel really mad.
I think they're a little sad.

I feel sorry for the homeless,
They have to sleep on the floor.
Not forgetting that they are poor,
They don't even have a front door.

Dominique Giddings (11)
The Nobel School, Stevenage

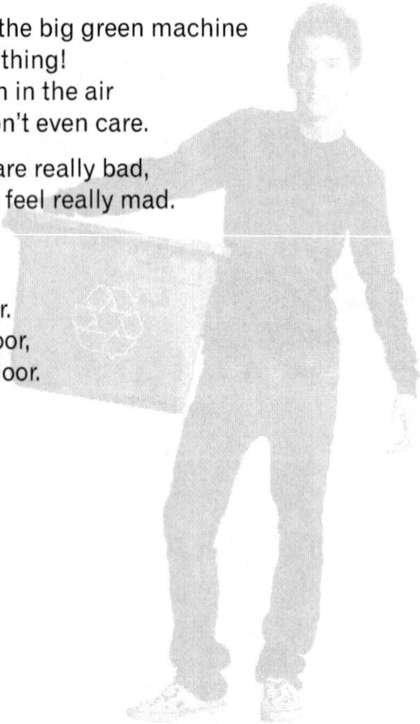

The Brightest Poppy

As you stand in Flanders fields and feel a tree of worry growing inside of you
You shakily hide and aim your gun and fire for victory and respect you know is yours
You feel a nasty mixture of worry and anger bubbling in your brain
You don't see the pellet coming at you until you turn and realise your time's up
You fall to the floor with deep disappointment but see blood slowly trickling everywhere
What you didn't know and see is how much people loved you
And now really miss your presence and they really did respect you
But most of all your memories in marvellous times are treasured and cherished
In a heart plated with gold and the brightest poppy hanging from the side
Many people now just get sad and blue and really can't abide
Very much how you died!

Ellie O'Brien (11)
Woodlands School, Basildon

Recycle

Recycle your rubbish, we can use it again.
Very soon it will be the end.
Clothes and shoes,
What you want to lose,
Bits and bobs you want to keep.
Help the people who are in need.

Chelsea Connelly (11)
Woodlands School, Basildon

Young Writers Information

We hope you have enjoyed reading this book - and that you will continue to enjoy it in the coming years.

If you like reading and writing poetry drop us a line, or give us a call, and we'll send you a free information pack.

Alternatively if you would like to order further copies of this book or any of our other titles, then please give us a call or log onto our website at www.youngwriters.co.uk

Young Writers Information
Remus House
Coltsfoot Drive
Peterborough
PE2 9JX
(01733) 890066